Love Prevails

One Couple's Story of Faith and Survival in the Rwandan Genocide

Jean Bosco Rutagengwa
with Daniel G. Groody

ORBIS BOOKS
Maryknoll, New York 10545

ORBIS BOOKS
Maryknoll, New York 10545

Fathers and Brothers
MARYKNOLL™

Founded in 1970, Orbis Books endeavors to publish works that enlighten the mind, nourish the spirit, and challenge the conscience. The publishing arm of the Maryknoll Fathers and Brothers, Orbis seeks to explore the global dimensions of the Christian faith and mission, to invite dialogue with diverse cultures and religious traditions, and to serve the cause of reconciliation and peace. The books published reflect the views of their authors and do not represent the official position of the Maryknoll Society. To learn more about Maryknoll and Orbis Books, please visit our website at www.maryknollsociety.org.

Manufactured in the United States of America

Library of Congress Cataloging-in-Publication Data

Names: Rutagengwa, Jean (Jean Bosco), author. | Groody, Daniel G., 1964-
    author.
Title: Love prevails : one couple's story of faith and survival in the
    Rwandan genocide / Jean Bosco Rutagengwa with Daniel G. Groody.
Description: Maryknoll, NY : Orbis Books, [2019]
Identifiers: LCCN 2018041100 (print) | LCCN 2018050655 (ebook) | ISBN
    9781608337767 (ebook) | ISBN 9781626983144 (pbk.)
Subjects: LCSH: Rutagengwa, Jean (Jean Bosco) | Genocide
    survivors–Rwanda–Biography. | Rwanda–History–Civil War, 1994–Personal
    narratives. | Genocide–Rwanda–History–20th century. |
    Rwandans–Religious life.
Classification: LCC DT450.443.R88 (ebook) | LCC DT450.443.R88 A3 2019
    (print)
    | DDC 967.57104/310922 [B] –dc23
LC record available at https://lccn.loc.gov/2018041100

To my parents, Francois and Febronie;
To my little sister Rose,
and my little brothers Regis and Jean Paul.

I miss you terribly.

To my extended family and friends gone too soon;
To all the victims of the genocide.

May this book be a sanctuary for the memory of your
dignified lives.

For my wife, Christine, and our children;
You are the reason I kept going.
I love you.

Contents

Foreword

Daniel G. Groody, CSC

In September of 2011, I was giving a talk at a regional Catholic Charities meeting in Rye, New Hampshire. The presentation sought to address the complex challenges posed by the global refugee crisis and how to think about the issue from a theological perspective. At one point during the discussion I said a few words about the Rwandan genocide of 1994, which produced more than two million refugees. Afterward a distinguished-looking African woman came up to me and thanked me for mentioning Rwanda. She herself was from Rwanda and now was living in the United States and working with Catholic Charities in the area. We talked for a while, and at the end of our conversation I thanked her for sharing some of her story and gave her my contact information. Before leaving I encouraged her to call me if she ever needed my assistance.

A few weeks later she called me back and went into her story in much more detail. She said that both she and her husband, Jean Bosco, had lived through the genocide together, and now—seventeen years later—they wanted to write something about it. "We have always wanted to tell our story," she added, "and we wanted to ask if you would help us with our reflection on where God was in the midst of what happened."

The invitation immediately struck me, but deep down I had some real hesitations. I said, "I would love to accompany you in the writing of this project. But in all sincerity, though trained as a theologian, I have no idea how to speak about God from this context." I had been working in the field of migrants, refugees, and theology for almost twenty years, but I had never dealt with a situation as dark and difficult as Rwanda.

In the one hundred days from April 7 to mid-July 1994, about one million people were killed in Rwanda's ethnic conflict. When the plane carrying Rwandan president Juvénal Habyarimana and Burundian president Cyprien Ntaryamira was shot down on April 6, 1994, the fragile peace accords in place ended, setting ablaze an all-out massacre. The genocide was orchestrated by members of the Hutu-majority government, who organized and backed militia groups such as the Interahamwe and Impuzamugambi. These rallied and organized Hutu civilians to arm themselves with machetes, clubs, and other blunt instruments to kill any Tutsi they came in contact with, including neighbors, coworkers and even family members. Before it was over, more than 70 percent of the Tutsi in the country were killed.

Christine and Jean Bosco were both Tutsis. They both had lived through the genocide. And they both sought refuge in the Hotel Mille Collines, also known as "Hotel Rwanda" from the Academy Award-winning Hollywood film of the same name. Though they lived through the same events depicted in the film, they had a different story to tell.

When Christine, Jean Bosco, and I first got together to talk about the book, it was the first Sunday after Ash Wednesday of 2012. We celebrated Mass together in their home, and the readings for the day spoke about Jesus's forty days in the desert. After the gospel reading we shared some reflections together, but Jean Bosco remained very quiet for some time. As he gathered his thoughts in light of the readings, he realized that Christine spent exactly forty days in the hotel during the genocide, from April 18 to May 27, 1994. From that moment forward, we explored not only the temptations in times of terror and fear but also the love and hope that strengthened them amidst those dark and evil days.

We worked together on the writing of their story for about a year. Reliving these events was particularly difficult for them, not only because they recalled the multiple times they narrowly escaped death but also because they had to remember many of their family members who suffered violent and brutal deaths. The deeper we got into the details, the more challenging the questions became—especially the theological questions. Where was God during the genocide? How could a good God allow such evil to happen, especially to so many innocent people? Why did they escape when others they knew didn't?

As the complex dimensions of the project expanded, I said to Jean Bosco and Christine, "Your story poses questions that are much bigger than the three of us, and we need more than our own insights." It became clear to me that we needed a community of people to reflect with us on the issues. In the following months we gathered theologians and other scholars, priests, and religious and friends and family members to read through the current manuscript and sort through a vast array of challenging issues. In December of 2013, we went back to Rwanda for ten days. Among those who joined us were Virgilio Elizondo, Jim Shannon, Fulata Moyo, Alan Hilliard, Colleen Cross, Bill Groody, Robert Ellsberg, and many practitioners and friends of Jean Bosco and Christine who lived through the genocide. In addition to writing this book, we worked together on a film called "Return to Rwanda" (https://vimeo.com/90597947), which chronicles some of the footage from this delegation, including interviews with some of these people on site in Rwanda.

One of the first places we visited was the parish where Christine grew up. It is called the Church of Ntarama, which now is one of six major centers in Rwanda that commemorate the 1994 genocide. On April 15, 1994, more than five thousand men, women, and children were killed at this site. When the murderous spree started, people fled to the churches for protection and refuge. But anticipating this move, the killers targeted and isolated these sanctuaries and then killed everyone inside. Now, years later, these churches have become memorial sites. Today the ceilings of the church are draped with the clothing of many who died there, and the machetes and blunt instruments used in the massacres are littered throughout this one-time house of worship. At the back are chilling displays of the bones of the victims, laid out on racks, in full view for everyone to see. Some of the skulls still have the spears thrust through them.

As we somberly walked through the area and contemplated the events, Christine was seeing more than skeletal remains; these were what were left of people and family members that she knew. Some of the killers came from the same communities, worshiped in the same church and even sang in the same choir as those they killed. How could this happen? How could it be, as one Nigerian bishop observed, that tribal blood was thicker than baptismal water?* Amidst the dank and lingering stench that still stains the space, a saying in Kinyarwanda stitched on purple cloth and draped over the altar summed up the incomprehensible reality in front of us: *Iyo Umenya Nawe Ukimenya Ntuba Waranyishe,* which means, "If you really knew me, and knew yourself, you wouldn't have killed me."

All of this took place in what at the time was the most "catholic" country in Africa. And one of the most beautiful geographically. To walk with Christine and Jean Bosco on their harrowing escapes and perilous moments felt at times like walking onto a stage and living through an action thriller. Their attempts to cheat death and foil their captives were as inspiring as they were frightening. As we went back to the "Swiss Village," where Jean Bosco hid on a roof to escape the killers, we learned of his daring interchanges with those who called for his life and the cunning and courageous adventures that led him eventually to safety inside the Hotel Milles Collines. But while he eventually managed to find some refuge in this hotel, a thin line of protection against the killers, he knew that the woman he loved was still at large—and at risk—in the city of Kigali. It was there that he had to make the choice that would define his life: Is it better to save your life when death surrounds you or to risk your life and even die for the sake of the one you love?

After walking with Christine and Jean Bosco through a land that was at the same time so beautiful but so tragic, we spent our last days in the hotel where Jean Bosco and Christine had taken their final refuge before being traded across enemy lines and finding protection. They stayed in the same hotel room where they had stayed some nineteen years before.

---

* For more on this subject, see Emmanuel Katongole, "A Blood Thicker than the Blood of Tribalism: Eucharist and Identity in African Politics," *Modern Theology* 30, no. 2 (April 2014): 319–25.

Christine's aunt, Sister Teya, a member of the
Little Sisters of Jesus.

During our delegation some of Christine's relatives also joined
us, and one of them was her aunt, an elderly nun named Sister Teya.
She was a very quiet woman, who barely uttered a word during
our whole time together. Toward the end, however, we asked her
to share some of her reflections. She first told us about where she
lived during the genocide and about a dog that lived with them, who
could be menacing and threatening. One day the killers came and
murdered a number of people in front of the Sisters and then buried
their bodies in their front yard. After they left, the Sisters were still
traumatized, yet the dog kept trying to get their attention by barking and growling, as if wanting to call their attention to something
going on outside. Eventually they found out he was trying to bring
their attention to the place where the bodies were buried because
one of the women in the grave was still alive. Though she suffered
life-altering injuries, she eventually survived and lived to tell her

story. Reflecting on this event, Sister Teya observed, "As mean as this animal was, he showed more humanity than the killers."

Before we were done, one of our group asked her one final question: "What have we learned from Rwanda that the rest of the world needs to hear?" She paused for a bit in silent reflection and then recalled a story that left an indelible impression on all of us. She said when the killing was happening and they came to her home, "I felt a fear and terror that is unlike anything I have ever felt. At that moment," she said, "Rwanda had fallen to the lowest point of our humanity. We had descended to our darkest depths. In the midst of that fear," she continued, "God did not take away my fear, but he met me in it and helped me go through it. And from this darkest point I felt an undeniable presence within me in which I had this conviction that God was calling me to be a messenger of light and hope and to put goodness back on its throne."

That message is at the heart of this book. As challenging and as difficult as it was to enter into the story of Rwanda's darkness in general, and into Jean Bosco's and Christine's journey in particular, what struck me the most about their story was that it was not simply a story about evil but about a love that is stronger than death. In other words, their story at its core is a love story: a love that goes beyond romance and self-preservation to laying down one's life and risking all for love of your friends. In the end, as we read about the Rwandan genocide through the eyes of Jean Bosco and Christine, we realize that the last word of this human tragedy was not death but life, not revenge but forgiveness, and not hatred but a love that prevails.

August 2018
University of Notre Dame

Historical Note

Rwanda is a small landlocked country in central/eastern Africa. Its fertile red soil supports an economy largely based on subsistence agriculture. It is known as the land of *mille collines*—"a thousand hills." Since 1994 it has also been known as the site of a savage genocide. In the course of a hundred days, Hutu militia, mostly armed with machetes and clubs, turned on their Tutsi neighbors, killing hundreds of thousands of men, women, and children. This book is a memoir of that experience. But it is a story rooted in a longer history.

For centuries Rwanda was a kingdom, led by kings chosen from a clan within the minority Tutsi ethnic group. For decades, Rwanda's colonial power, Belgium, relied on the king and his entourage to assert its influence and solidify its grip on the country. The Belgians established their administrative headquarters in my home town of Nyanza, which was the capital of the kingdom. At first, they found a people united under the authority of the king, speaking the same language, believing in one God, and sharing the same culture. But gradually the Belgians developed theories that Tutsi, who were cow herders for the most part, were more intelligent and more refined than their fellow compatriots, the Hutu, who were farmers. They believed that Tutsi had "nobler," more naturally "aristocratic" features than the Hutu. The Belgian colonials even went as far as measuring Rwandans' noses and other physical dimensions, asserting that Tutsi were taller and had longer and narrower noses, as opposed to Hutu, who were found to be shorter and with broader noses. Over the years, their comparative analysis led them to believe that the Tutsi were a distinct "race" that originated from Abyssinia—that is, Ethiopia—who had, despite being a minority group, conquered Rwanda and politically dominated the Hutu majority.

Eventually, the Belgians conducted a census and issued identity cards, identifying the ethnic group to which each cardholder belonged. Long after the end of colonial rule, these identity cards would continue to define the divide between the two main ethnic groups in Rwanda.

In the late 1950s, the system of monarchy was challenged by a rising political movement formed by Hutu politicians, who advocated for power for the Hutu majority. Eventually the Belgian colonials changed their attitude toward the Tutsi elite and turned their support to the Hutu movement, which conducted a bloody revolution in 1959 that ended the system of monarchy and led in the early 1960s to the formation of a republic. Unfortunately, the change of the political system did nothing to bring unity. Instead, Rwanda's governance since then was based on the idea of political dominance by the Hutu ethnic majority over the Tutsi minority, and authorities used every means, including violence and intimidation, to maintain that political order.

The Hutu uprising sparked the very first ethnic conflict in Rwanda's history, resulting in the deaths of thousands of Tutsi civilians and causing the exile of a hundred thousand more to neighboring countries between 1959 and 1961. A new cycle of violence continued after independence in 1962. Tutsi refugees, claiming their right to return and to participate in the governance of the country, began organizing attacks on Hutu military positions inside Rwanda. Such attacks occurred between 1962 and 1967. Unfortunately, these attacks led to retaliatory massacres by the Rwandan Hutu army of a large number of Tutsi civilians still living in Rwanda. Consequently, more Tutsis continued to flee the country.

The "First Republic," after the country's independence in 1962, was led by President Gregoire Kayibanda, a Hutu from the South. He was determined to keep Tutsi refugees living in the neighboring countries from returning to Rwanda. A few who returned were jailed. The government used the identity card as a tool to exclude the Tutsi population living in Rwanda from education, public administration, and political aspirations.

When the Kayibanda regime was removed from power in a 1973 coup staged by Army chief Major General Juvénal Habyarimana, the new president presented himself as a uniter, declaring since day one of the coup that the country "could no longer tolerate ethnic discrimination." He promised peace, unity, and economic stability. Habyarimana's assurance was a relief for the Tutsi population and many moderate Hutus. A practicing Catholic, the president won favor among the predominately Catholic population, along with support from the clergy and even the Vatican. He favored a "development ideology" and unveiled plans to achieve economic self-sufficiency, build infrastructure, and open Rwanda to international cooperation. The country started to play an important role on the regional stage and developed strong ties with European countries, particularly France.

But only a couple of years into the "Second Republic," Habyarimana began to implement policies that mirrored the discriminatory practices of his predecessor. He reenforced the system of quotas applied by the previous regime to limit education and job opportunities available to the Tutsi population; and he was even more determined than his predecessor to keep refugees out of the country, making it impossible for families to reunite.

In 1990, Tutsi exiles organized as the Rwandan Patriotic Front organized an attack on Rwanda from their base in Uganda. This was the beginning of a war that lasted until 1993 with the signing of a peace agreement. Hard-line members of the Hutu government opposed President Habyarimana's signing of the peace agreement. On April 6, 1994, a plane carrying the president was shot down as it approached Kigali airport. This event was the signal for the genocide to begin.

Prologue

I could sense fear in my fiancée's voice. Fear as I had never felt it before. "They are here; they are surrounding the house," she was whispering, her voice trembling. Her words through the phone line conveyed a deep sense of despair and panic that sent a chill down my spine. I knew who "they" were: the killers. In my mind I could picture them, advancing quietly and confidently, like hunters closing in on their prey, knowing it has no chance of escape. What I had feared was happening. And there was nothing I could do right now. I blamed myself for not having left this place while I could, taking my fiancée with me to safety. But who knew things were going to be this bad? Now the streets were closed to traffic, with road-blocks everywhere, and the city of Kigali was in a state of chaos, held hostage by armed soldiers and merciless militiamen whose killing instincts had reached the height of insanity. I did not know then that all the ingredients were ready for a total ethnic cleansing, a full-blown genocide. I was about to say something to reassure my fiancée when I heard a shot, followed by a scream; then the phone line went dead. I screamed with rage, the phone receiver still in my hand, not knowing what to do. Slowly, I got down on my knees and began to pray.

PART I

Life

Beside my father, Francois, on December
26, 1993, the day of my wedding engagement
ceremony.

1

The Last Gathering

The day after Christmas 1993, the morning sun rose in a cloud-less sky, promising to brighten a day that will forever hold a special place in my heart. This was the day of my official engagement to my fiancée, Christine. I had alerted every family member and all my friends to reserve the day for the special occasion. They all came in large numbers, and we descended in force to the Bugesera region in southeastern Rwanda, where my future in-laws lived.

My family and friends arrived late morning at Christine's house in Bugesera. Her family and guests equally matched our number, which was in the hundreds. Her parents' modest house had been renovated for the occasion, and the front yard was covered with a large tent under which chairs and tables had been arranged. All those attending the ceremony had arrayed themselves in their best outfits, in order to do honor to the day. Women were dressed in their beautiful traditional dresses made of soft and colorful silk material and consisting of a long wrap skirt and a sash that drapes over their shoulders. Younger women wore jewelry around their necks while the oldest wore the traditional crown of motherhood, worn only on special occasions. Most men were dressed in dark suits and ties, a style borrowed from the Western culture that won over the Rwandan men's traditional dress after the colonial era.

We were welcomed warmly by Christine's family, and they made us feel like royalty. We were seated opposite the side of the bride's family. The elders started exchanging pleasantries as they sipped

their beer or banana wine. I looked around and realized in amazement that my parents had invited almost everyone I knew growing
up in our small town of Nyanza in the South. They included teachers, civil servants, local store owners, and farmers. All my own
invitees were there too. Our guests mingled like one big, happy
family, engaging in small talk and laughing as if they had known
one another for a long time.

After a moment, the master of ceremonies requested our attention and said that the guest of honor wanted to address the audience. At this signal, my mother's uncle, Theophile Sebalinda,
whom we all regarded as the patriarch of our family, stood, extending his tall frame, while the place went quiet. This marked the
beginning of the show—a show indeed, for the Rwandan traditional engagement ceremony is a play. Though everyone knows
that the true engagement is sealed between the two young lovers, the matter still has to go through a ritual of negotiations and
agreements between the two families before becoming valid and
official. The groom's family must go beyond the simple act of asking for the bride's hand in marriage. They must strive to demon-
strate why their son should be accepted. On the other hand, the
bride's family must not give up their darling daughter too easily.
Their strategy is to delay their response, buying time for a supposedly thoughtful, wise decision, or offering alternatives. They
may also choose to go on the offensive, raising concerns over the
other family's "faulty behavior" and "imperfections." Since no one
is perfect, fault is always found, forcing the groom's family to prove
their nobility of character and worthiness. The entire exchange is
conducted in a friendly and courteous atmosphere, and the words
spoken must carry a poetic resonance. Almost none of the stories
told by either side is true, but what matters is not their accuracy
but the cleverness and finesse of the arguments. It is a verbal game
of chess, in which the goal is not to capture the "king" but to win
over the hearts of the audience. The ending is always happy, and
there are no losers.

No one played this wedding game better than Sebalinda, a living museum of culture. He knew very well the basics of the speech
protocol. A great traditional engagement speech starts with polite-

ness and generalities, aimed to earn the audience's trust and openness and to prepare everyone's mind for the request to follow. A speech that goes straight to the point would be considered tactless and unworthy.

Sebalinda started by thanking Christine's family for the cordial reception and praised his counterpart on the other side, Jean Berchmans Kaboyi, who represented Christine's family, for being a good keeper of the great Rwandan tradition of hospitality and for passing them on to the younger generation. Then he embarked on an imaginary tale of a long and exemplary friendship between the two families. He said that for centuries, the two families had built strong relationships and had intermarried. "Many of our daughters and sisters married within your family, and so did yours on our side," he added, reinforcing the assertion that the connections were legendary and unbreakable. He elaborated with stories and examples of the historical interrelations, past and recent, as the audience nodded in agreement, encouraging him to proceed with confidence. None of these stories was true, but again, this was a performance in which everyone was happy to play along.

"We have traveled to your beautiful Bugesera region to continue the great tradition of love started by our ancestors," he continued, now arriving at the true purpose of the visit. He spoke about love as I had never heard it before, describing how it envelopes the lovers in its warm mist, then spreads within their surroundings, carrying powerful emotions that bring people together. When the time came to ask for Christine's hand in marriage, he took the speech to a higher level. He made the commitment that if ever "we are found worthy of her hand," the lovely bride would be cherished, respected, and always loved.

No doubt he was smooth and skilled. He chose his words effortlessly, drawing them from the ancient, rich Kinyarwanda language. The audience watched his performance with great admiration, and upon concluding he received a round of applause that lasted several minutes.

I caught a glimpse of my father, a smile on his face, whispering something to my mother. I could guess what he told her: "Very well said." And she nodded in agreement. My parents were living

On the day of my wedding engagement ceremony, my mother's uncle
Theophile, my mother, Febronie,
and her aunt Marguerite.

the best part of their lives. Just recently my sister Chantal had
married, and now she was expecting her first child; soon my parents would become grandparents. And now, with this wedding,
two good reasons for them to be ecstatic.

Next to my mother was her Aunt Marguerite and Sebalinda's
wife, Immaculee, a lovely grandmother with an eternal smile. All
around us, pride was on every face. My aunts Epiphanie and Iphigénie, usually very reserved, were now cheerful. Iphigénie, who
always threw jokes at me, looked at me through her big eyeglasses
and gave me a thumbs up. Next to them sat my younger sisters,
Julienne and Rose, wearing colorful dresses, my cousin Philippe,
and my uncle Hildegarde, who was wearing a black bow tie on a
white shirt, as he always did on special occasions. My younger
brother Regis was in the back and looked busy, helping the cam-
eraman with something. A handy teenage boy, always eager to
help, Regis had grown into a smart and disciplined young man; I
had high hopes for him.

My sister Chantal and her husband, Joseph, were sitting in the
row just behind me. Joseph was my best friend from high school

and college. We were part of a group of very close friends who
had become inseparable. The other three members of that group,
Constantin Cyubahiro, Aloys Niyoyita, and Godefroid Ritararenga,
were seated next to Joseph with their wives. They were making all
sorts of comments, mostly funny. Godefroid was the funniest; he
cracked a joke and we all broke up laughing.

On the opposite side from us were members of Christine's family and many of her friends. I had met several of them. Her father,
Straton Mutabaruka, mother Nathalie, and uncle Laurent Kayijamahe sat quietly in the first row. Some of her eight siblings, aunts,
and cousins could be seen in the audience, while others were
inside the house to keep the bride company.

Minutes later the master of ceremonies requested silence
again and introduced the next speaker. Jean Berchmans Kaboyi,
a respected teacher in a local elementary school and a friend of
Christine's father, stood and asked the audience to give his counterpart Sebalinda another round of applause. He thanked him and
his entourage for bringing a message of love and friendship. In his
brief but eloquent address, he confirmed the strong relationships
and the long tradition of intermarriage between the two families.

"Dear Sebalinda," he began, "our friendship is so deep there is
nothing in my possession I can refuse to your family; our ancestors have taught us to share joy, happiness, and certainly love. I
will not be the first to break this great tradition." Anyone unfa-
miliar with the Rwandan tradition would have thought we had
easily secured his consent for Christine's hand. But I knew our
wish was still far from being fulfilled. "Unfortunately," he continued, "the bride whom you are requesting in marriage is not available," Kaboyi said. Christine, he claimed, had recently decided to
become a nun. He said this with a sincere expression worthy of
belief. And it was indeed believable, for religious vocations ran in
Christine's family. Just behind Kaboyi sat Christine's aunt, Sister
Teya of the Little Sisters of Jesus. "You are screwed," my friend
Godefroid whispered to me.

"But I would be saddened to see you go home empty handed,"
he said, "so I will not let this happen." He continued: "Although
Christine is not available, we have in our family several equally

beautiful brides, imbibed with our traditional values of kindness, honesty, and unconditional love."

As he was saying this, two little girls, both under age seven, were escorted through the seats and stopped in front of Sebalinda. This was another element of the Rwandan wedding tradition. You can never hope to win the bride you came for on your first attempt; instead, you are offered alternatives that are aimed to test your patience. "I certainly hope you will find in these beautiful ladies the bride you are looking for," Kaboyi concluded, before sitting down amidst laughter and amused comments from the audience.

I knew Sebalinda was prepared for the challenge, but I wondered how he was going to respond. He rose from his seat, a big smile on his face. He could not flatly reject his counterpart's proposal; he wouldn't dare. But he needed to bring the conversation back to the actual bride he and his entourage had traveled for. "I knew this was my lucky day," he said, with surprising conviction. "Thank you for extending your family's love to us through these adorable future brides. We like them, and I can assure you we will be back when the time is right."

Then he spoke about the "nun" situation. "I understand one of your daughters chose to join the religious life as a nun. I applaud her, and I congratulate your entire family. I will not do anything that will go against the will of God, which I and every member of my family respect profoundly. You raised your daughter well, and I'm glad God chose her. But I came to ask for her sister's hand in marriage, not for hers." He paused to let his words sink in. "So let's clear up what seems to be a misunderstanding. We came for *Christine*, not for *Christiana,*" he added.

There was a little commotion on the bride's side, and Kaboyi was seen consulting with his immediate entourage. Then he rose, his face assuming an apologetic countenance. He regretfully acknowledged his mistake, blaming the confusion on his being "too old." "You are correct as always," he graciously conceded to Sebalinda. "It is your lucky day, indeed, for I do not see any reason not to grant your wishes; you have my word, the bride is yours, you deserve her." A warm round of applause followed. However, I knew there must be a "but."

"But," continued Kaboyi, "I spoke only for myself. Our child has uncles, aunts, and cousins. We need to hear from them as well." The wider family had to have their say in the matter. At this point everybody tensed, or at least feigned to tense, for the ceremony could be further delayed if anyone from the family raised an issue. But no one did. No one found fault. All was good.

"Dear Sebalinda, either you are a saint or you bribed my entire family," Kaboyi jokingly commented. Then he solemnly declared that he and the entire family had no objection to give Christine's hand in marriage. As expected, the crowd erupted in a storm of applause. More drinks were served and the two families relaxed, exchanged pleasantries, and shared laughter. Part one of the wedding ceremony was concluded. Part two, the presentation of the dowry, would follow.

Unlike in many other cultures, the dowry in Rwanda is brought by the groom's family. It is a wedding present given to honor the bride and her family. In the Rwandan tradition it consists of one or several cows. Traditionally, the engagement and the dowry ceremonies are not supposed to be held the same day. But for convenience and practical reasons, nowadays the two ceremonies are held the same day. And this is exactly what Sebalinda and Kaboyi had agreed to do.

When Kaboyi stood, he did not ask for anything. He eloquently spoke of this part of the culture, indirectly asking Sebalinda whether he intended to honor in any way the bride he was just given, and "whose other name," he hinted, "is _Mukobwajana_— 'worthy of a hundred cows.'" Speaking in parable, he tried to sound as if we were not asking about the dowry, although, of course, he was. "Whoever has ears to hear should listen," he mysteriously concluded, before taking his seat.

"I even have big ears," Sebalinda joked. Then, in a more serious tone, he said he came prepared. He beautifully spoke of the cattle our family owns, which, he said with exaggeration, consists of handsome breeds rarely seen in the country. He added that he brought hundreds with him for the bride's family to choose from. The truth was, my family had brought two cows, which was an above average number (the norm was only one cow), though well below the number Sebalinda claimed to have brought. But again, the wedding ceremony in Rwanda is a play, where exaggeration is allowed for the sake of everyone's entertainment.

Two cowherds, one on each side, were called and instructed to go down to the valley to choose the best breeds. Moments later they came back, supposedly coming from the valley with their report. In fact they did not go beyond the backyard. The cows my family brought were breeds of mixed races, and I knew they were handsome, but when one of the cowherds described them, I thought he had seen holy, golden creatures. He used words I had never heard before, painting a breathtaking view of what he had just seen. Then the cowherd on my family's side started singing the "cows' names," a pure expression of the importance given to cattle in the Rwandan wedding tradition. His voice was smooth and beautiful, and his words were metaphors that expressed love, beauty, harmony, and generosity. People watched his performance in amazement.

The last part of the ceremony, which consists of introducing the groom and the bride, is optional. Although the engagement is about them, it is not between them; it is between the two families. For that reason, throughout the preceding ceremony, my name had not even been mentioned.

But Sebalinda couldn't introduce me until he was asked to do so. When Kaboyi issued the invitation, Sebalinda introduced me to great applause. I took time to hug almost everyone in Christine's family, starting with her parents, uncles, and aunts. New glasses were brought and beer was served. After a moment, Sebalinda politely asked if he could have the honor to see the bride. Kaboyi did not object but asked to be given some time to get the bride ready. I could feel the anticipation building among the crowd. The arrival of the bride is, indeed, the most spectacular moment of the engagement ceremony.

All eyes turned when Christine and her bridesmaids arrived, slowly advancing in line on the rhythm of a beautiful Rwandan song. They were dressed in gorgeous traditional dresses made out of soft, clear silk fabric. They wore simple but chic jewelry that brought life to their outfits. They carried gifts for my family. Their arrival lifted the spirits and added joy to an already festive atmosphere. Christine greeted first the elders from my family, hugging them and offering a warm smile. She served them wine, a traditional way of showing hospitality and expressing respect. Then she gave me a long embrace that received a warm applause from the audience. We exchanged gifts before she and the bridesmaids took their seats on my left. It looked as though the festivities were just beginning. But soon it would be time to part ways.

Sebalinda knew when to say goodbye, and how. One does not leave a Rwandan ceremony without giving a valid reason. In another eloquent address, he first apologized for interrupting the festivities, and then thanked the host family for their hospitality and for the trust put in our family. He regretted having to say goodbye but explained why: we needed to bring the good news to other family members back home. Kaboyi feigned surprise, and insisted on spending a little more time with the guests. This was the tradition. One never lets his guests slip away at their first request. Sebalinda knew he would need to insist, and eventually Kaboyi "reluctantly" accepted. We were given some good wine and soft drinks to bring with us. "I would be remiss if any of you suffered from thirst on your way back home," Kaboyi added. After the two men exchanged the last words, our photographer gathered us and took the last shots of the day, immortalizing this precious moment.

As we exited the premises, it started raining. "A sign of good luck," someone said. My engagement to Christine had now received the blessings of our families. And I had no doubt we had God's consent as well. It was the most precious Christmas gift one could wish for.

None of us knew that this was to be the last family gathering.

2

Rwanda: A Land of Life, Love, and War

Three months later . . .

On the evening of April 6, 1994, I was living a dream. I was preparing for my wedding, while also looking forward to embracing an exciting new professional career abroad.

I was driving home after dropping off my fiancée at her home in Rugenge, a section of the capital, Kigali, and I reflected on my good fortune. The darkness of that quiet spring night was getting thicker, and I had to focus on the road to avoid driving into a ditch. My old Peugeot 305 was like an old dog, well on in years but loyal. Though its shock absorbers were bad, it was not struggling as usual with the dirt road. Maybe it shared my festive mood. As often happened when I was behind the wheel, my mind drifted back to the divine encounter of a year and a half ago that warmed my heart and captured my soul as never before.

The occasion was actually a tragedy. In the summer of 1992, I was attending the wake of a very lovely woman, Melanie, whose husband, Laurent Kayijamahe, was a friend of my parents. Melanie had been a devoted mother of seven and a devout Catholic who was a beloved member of the community. She was only fifty-two and had passed away unexpectedly. Friends and relatives had gathered at the house to present their condolences to the bereaved family.

Kayijamahe's niece, Christine, arrived at the house late in the afternoon, coming from the northern city of Gisenyi, where she attended college. She had been in high school the last time I had seen her, and I remembered her as a shy and good-mannered young lady. Now, at twenty-five, she was an elegant and confident woman. As I watched her advancing among the small crowd gathered in the front yard, I forgot for an instant that I was at a wake. When I looked at her I felt a sudden shock, as if I had been struck by lightning. Something clicked in me—something strong, warm, and irreversible. Her natural and innocent beauty took my breath away. Was this love? It was a feeling that I still can't describe, but I knew it was special. At that moment I felt that if she would ever join hands with me I would never let her go.

Weeks later, when I invited her out on a date, I would discover that there was more to Christine than physical beauty. She manifested the grace and dignity of the ideal Rwandan woman; I was amazed by her maturity and her down-to-earth attitude. That date became the first of many. We went out as often as we could, and we gradually embarked on a strong, romantic journey together, one that seemed to go into the very depths of our being, to the core of our very souls. With each passing day our love grew stronger. I was inspired by the strength and depth of her Catholic faith, a humble, sensitive, and gentle faith that spoke volumes. She was the ideal companion, full of grace and wisdom, caring, responsible, and trustworthy.

Eventually, I asked her to marry me. Our engagement occurred in a restaurant on the outskirts of Kigali. The bright stars in the dark sky and the soft breeze of the evening made a perfect romantic setting. I proposed privately, the old-fashioned Rwandan way, with no fanfare. I was nervous and couldn't find my words. Kinyarwanda is not known to be the language of romance, so I borrowed some words from French. But I spoke from my heart and spilled out what was at its very bottom. Her soft, warm response filled my whole being with light, as it conveyed the consent I was dying to hear.

Although I had secured Christine's consent, tradition required that my family officially ask for her hand in marriage on my behalf. I had already introduced her to my family and to every one of my closest friends. They all fell in love with her and promised to be there whenever we decided to get officially engaged.

I was smiling at the thought of those sweet times as I approached the Kiyovu residential area where I lived. But my smile faded as a military truck full of armed soldiers passed by, a reminder that my country was in the midst of a war. Slowing down to let the truck pass, I watched it disappear down the street. Had fighting resumed after a recent cease-fire?

For the last three and a half years, the Rwandan military, composed primarily of Hutu, the majority ethnic group, had been unsuccessfully fighting along the northern border against rebels of the Rwandan Patriotic Front (RPF), a political movement formed by refugees living in neighboring countries. These refugees, mostly of the Tutsi minority ethnic group, had fled the country decades ago when Rwanda was undergoing violent political changes.

The war, now in its fourth year, had caught off guard the entire country, as well as its European allies, who regarded Rwanda as a stable and peaceful nation. Perhaps no one wanted to admit that this beautiful land of a "thousand hills" and valleys, often referred to by foreigners as the "Switzerland of Africa," and by locals as the "land of milk and honey," could see its unity fade in discord and surrender to the ugliness of violence.

But the conflict had exposed an abscess that had been growing over the past three decades. A postcolonial history of discrimination and violence against the minority Tutsi population had created waves of refugees. Since taking power in a coup twenty years before, Major General Juvénal Habyarimana, a Hutu from the North, had imposed an iron rule on the country, institutionalizing a dictatorship that suppressed the rights of the average Rwandan.

The RPF's main goals were to force President Habyarimana to let all refugees freely return to Rwanda (which he had vehemently refused to do), and to open the Rwandan political space to more than one party. The launch of the war by the RPF sparked violence against the Tutsi minority group, to which Christine and I belonged, and also against moderate Hutu who wanted to embrace democratic reforms. The Habyarimana government did everything it could, resorting to intimidation and even murder, to cling to absolute power and prevent change. It labeled us, the Tutsi, as accomplices of the RPF, and the moderate Hutu as traitors. The violence was mostly attributed to the Interahamwe, a paramilitary Hutu militia created and financed by the Habyarimana regime, but the army had also played a role in the killings, thereby implanting in the mind of many residents a permanent fear of men in uniform.

Now the sight of the army truck moving down the street revived my own fears. I was often apprehensive about bumping into armed soldiers coming from the frontline; the Rwandan army had lost many battles against the rebels of the RPF and had often retaliated against Tutsi civilians.

Without any incident I reached my home on Kayuku Street in Kiyovu, the central residential area of the capital. I parked in the backyard and remained in my car for a few long moments, contemplating my plans for the future. Very soon I hoped to start a new job at the Preferential Trade Area, a regional economic organization based in Lusaka, Zambia, representing about twenty African nations. Administrative formalities for my employment were under way. I planned to return in the summer for my wedding with Christine. There were still three months separating us from our big day and our plans to leave Rwanda. What could happen in the meantime was anyone's guess. In the past three and a half years of war, we had seen many people leaving the country for reasons of safety. But still, most people believed the worst was behind us. Just recently, the parties in conflict had signed a peace agreement; the United Nations had sent a peace-keeping mission led by Romeo Dallaire, a Canadian general. The sight of these UN "blue helmets" patrolling the streets of Kigali was certainly reassuring. Political reforms were under way, with plans for a new government to be formed by several political parties. Certainly, we were on the right path for lasting peace. So it seemed.

As I sat in my car on that quiet night, I tried to push away the thought of war and violence. Right now I wanted to focus on happy events. Part of me felt that everything would be all right. It was an inner voice that had always carried me through anxious times—a soothing, warm voice I was born with. A gift from God. *"Everything will be all right,"* it always said.

I could not have been more wrong.

3

The Beginning of the End

The telephone was ringing as I entered my house. It was my neighbor, Therese, a medical doctor at the Kigali hospital. She had never actually called me before, and I was surprised that she should call so late. What could be wrong?

"Did you hear what happened?" she asked, with a shaky voice.

My heart beat faster, sensing some sort of trouble.

"What do you mean? I just got home and did not get to put the radio on," I said.

"It's not on the radio yet," she explained. "My husband just called and told me the bad news. There has been a grave incident." She paused and then added, "The president has been killed. His plane was shot down tonight."

The news took a long while to sink in. I knew the ramifications of this event could have serious consequences for the already fragile state of the political situation. Therese did not have any specific details, but I could tell she was scared. After she hung up, I stood there, lost in thought, the phone receiver still in my hands.

My cousin Philippe was in the living room watching a movie. Noticing my expression, he paused the VCR and stared at me. "What's wrong?" he asked. I explained what Therese had just told me. My younger sister Julienne and my cousin Murekatete emerged from the kitchen with an anxious look on their faces. Murekatete looked more worried; she was visiting for a few days and was planning to return to her home in the South the next morning. With Therese's news it did not seem likely that buses would be leaving town.

"Come on! Do not pay attention to this, they are lying as usual," Philippe said. "They are just looking for another opportunity to throw in prison all these political opponents who are giving them a hard time," he added, before resuming his movie.

I knew my cousin did not believe his own words. He was born in exile in the neighboring country of Burundi after his parents had fled violence against Tutsis in the 1950s. Life in Burundi, as Philippe described it, was challenging for his family and for Rwandan refugees in general. They faced discrimination everywhere, particularly in the job market, with no option of becoming Burundian citizens. After college, Philippe had returned to Rwanda to claim his identity. After a lengthy process, he obtained an identity card, then later found a job as a math teacher in high school. Having reached some measure of comfort and success, he didn't want to imagine that anything could disturb his tranquil life and newfound sense of security. But he knew better.

Suddenly, a huge explosion tore the entire neighborhood, and everybody in the house plunged to the floor. For the next hour, the whole area was shaken by the sound of gunfire. The furor of the shooting stopped for about ten minutes and then started again. I figured we would not sleep in our beds that night and thought the safest place was in the hallway. I pulled out a mattress, and we all stayed there. The hallway was small, and we were huddled up close to each other, breathing heavily, all of us scared. I could feel the adrenaline in my veins, causing my heart to beat at an alarming rate. All night we heard bullets whistle over our heads, as if the shooting were in our own backyard. I prayed to God to keep us safe. We did not sleep at all.

What was happening? Was it a coup? What would this situation mean for us, and how long would it last? Though I had no answer to any of these questions, I knew the president's death could change everything, and fast. If soldiers were shooting, it meant that people were dying.

Of course, I could not stop thinking about Christine. What if I didn't see her again? Unfortunately, I couldn't directly reach her. There was no phone in the annex where she lived with friends from college. I usually called her through her landlord, who lived in the main house in front of the annex. But I decided not to bother anyone at that late hour. I would contact her in the morning.

I spent the night asking myself why I had not left the country while I could. In the past months the situation in Rwanda had deteriorated, and life in the country was often troubled by news of massacres of Tutsi civilians and of random killings of political opponents. Just a month and half before, the situation in Kigali had become volatile, following the shooting of the minister of public works, a moderate Hutu from the opposition. In retaliation his supporters had killed the leader of the "Coalition for the Defense of the Republic" (CDR), an extremist party that advocated for a "pure Hutu" nation.

Several zones of Kigali, including Christine's neighborhood in Rugenge, and the Remera area, where my sister Chantal lived, literally exploded into unprecedented violence. Most of this was committed by CDR's paramilitary wing, "Impuzamugambi," and fueled by the "Radio Television Libre des Milles Collines" (RTLM), a private extremist radio station financed and ideologically supported by politicians and businessmen from the president's region in the North. Tutsi and moderate Hutu were the ultimate targets of CDR and RTLM. Hundreds of them hastily left their homes and fled to safer areas.

Christine and four of her siblings who lived with her were forced to flee their neighborhood that day. She went to stay with friends, while her siblings came to my house. That same day Chantal gave birth to her son at the Kigali hospital, but she couldn't go home to Remera; the streets there were too dangerous. As I lived only a couple of miles from the hospital, she and baby Steve came to my house to stay with us temporarily. For several days it was chaos in the city.

Sister Teya, Christine's aunt, had urged me on more than one occasion to consider leaving the country, and Christine had agreed. *"You need to leave now,"* they had both told me again and again with insistence. Sister Teya had seen much in her lifetime. She had lived through the political turmoil that shook the country in the 1960s and caused many deaths among the Tutsi population. She was very protective of my relationship with her niece and had given us her heartfelt blessings. But she was increasingly concerned about my safety. There were rumors in the capital that extremists had compiled lists of people, mainly Tutsi, to be eliminated. "Men are the most at risk," she had told me. "Think of any safe place and go; leave Christine and your future plans in the hands of God."

I had been hesitant and uncertain of what to do. I did not know exactly where to go, nor did I have the means to make a living abroad. The only country I could go to was Burundi, Rwanda's southern neighbor, where several members of my extended family had fled ethnic persecution in the early 1960s. But Burundi was itself in the midst of a civil war. Also, now that I was awaiting the completion of administrative formalities to start my new career abroad, getting away from Rwanda could complicate the process. But I knew Teya and Christine were right; anything could happen at any moment. My mind had been working hard to figure out the best option that would provide safety without requiring risky adventures. I had not yet found that option. Maybe it did not exist.

After those first stressful days, calm had eventually returned to the capital. RTLM continued to broadcast its hateful messages, but people in general eventually ignored them. We continued to hear rumors that extremists had made lists of people to be eliminated, but that was hard to believe. Who in his right mind would carry out such evil plans? There were individuals in the army and in the intelligence rumored to be responsible for murdering innocent civilians, but people in general did not think that evil could prevail over the forces of good. After all, Rwanda was a majority Christian nation, with an impressive church presence. The Rwandan political elite had deep roots in the church and close ties with its leadership. Most importantly, these politicians feared criticism from the international community on whose financial support the country depended. Despite ongoing tensions, aggravated by hate media, there was finally a path and hope for peace.

Now, the shooting down of the president's plane had caught me off guard, throwing cold water on my hopes. I was not sure what this meant for the country. But I felt that something was about to go horribly wrong, and it awakened memories of fear and vulnerability I had had ever since I was a child.

4

Strangers in Our Native Land

Iwas nine years old when I learned of my ethnicity, that I was a Tutsi. This came with a frightening sensation of being different, isolated, and vulnerable. In fact, a single incident that occurred in the spring of 1973 opened my eyes to the sad reality of ethnic discrimination.

I remember walking to school with my younger sister Chantal and older brother Aimable. The morning was foggy but ordinary, with the same routines as for any other day. The mist made it difficult to see ten feet ahead. We could only see the tip of the Muhabura volcano, which stood tall in the horizon. We had just finished eating breakfast, which consisted of hot Indian tea prepared by my mother and a slice of white bread, to which I had applied a thick layer of margarine. We were happy-go-lucky children who were surrounded only by love and who saw the world as an exciting and wonderful place. We had moved to that part of northeastern Rwanda a year ago from the South, and this was my last quarter of fourth grade. It was a five-mile walk if we followed the street, but we had a shortcut that would take off a couple of miles.

We descended the hill through a field of green peas, still wet with dew drops, and then traversed the woods following a narrow path. In front of us there suddenly appeared a man carrying a machete. I knew this was not unusual; a machete was just a farmer's tool used to cut wood. Still it always terrified me, and I hated that kind of encounter. I could see my siblings were scared as well. We instantly ran into the woods to let the man pass. *"Muhumure"* ("do not be afraid"), the man said as he passed, visibly sorry for having frightened us. Thank God he was a good man. I was able to breathe again. Soon we reached the main street that would take us to our school, which was located right behind the church. The fog had started to lift and we could see ahead of us. The sandy surface of the street did not make it easy to walk, particularly when one walked on bare feet. I had the privilege of owning a pair of shoes, but since other children from my school did not have any, I couldn't put them on; my parents did not want me to look different. My siblings and I could wear shoes only for Mass on Sundays. We passed the military barracks on our right, where I could see soldiers in dark pants, black boots, and white or grey sweatshirts doing their morning workout, singing and shouting. I had always found their manners violent, and that morning was no different. But I thought I saw something else in the soldiers' eyes: a hostile and unfriendly disposition. I guess I assumed the military was supposed to be that way, so I kept walking.

Along the street were aligned small brick houses where government employees, particularly judges, hospital personnel, and high school teachers lived with their families. One of the families that lived there were our friends. I had on more than one occasion stopped by their home to relay a message from my parents, and I sometimes played soccer with their youngest son, who was my age. The area was usually quiet at this early morning hour, but not that day. As my siblings and I approached, I saw a group of people surrounding the house, brandishing machetes and shouting. Suddenly, someone smashed the door open, and the family's teenage son came out. He was still in his pajamas. He was holding a big stick, and he started fighting with the assailants. My siblings and I could not bear to watch the fighting, so we ran as fast as we could. I did not understand why they were fighting, but I sensed something grave was happening. When we stopped half a mile away, I was out of breath. My heart was beating so hard that I pressed on my chest to keep it steady. My entire body was shaking from fear.

The elementary school was just behind the Catholic church, and before the church was the town's secondary school, a boarding school sponsored by the church. Again, this was usually a quiet place, especially early in the morning. But not today. The students were out, shouting and visibly agitated. Some were hanging notices on trees alongside the road, and people were reading what was written on the notices. I was curious as well and went off to check out what everybody was reading. The first lines stated something like, "*The following people are enemies of our country and have been expelled from our school.*" There were several sheets that listed people's names. The only name that I recognized was that of my mother's cousin who was a teacher at the high school. I was about to leave when a group of these students came and surrounded me. One of the boys said, menacingly brandishing his fist: "Go away, you little snake; we know who you are!" Confused and frightened, I left the place as fast as I could.

We know who you are! What did he mean? I felt like all my movements were being watched by an invisible, evil spirit. But I knew I had done nothing wrong, and certainly my parents did not. When I reached my school, I saw a group of teachers talking in low voices. Definitely something unusual was happening. During school recess, some children were talking about the events of the day. They were saying, "Tutsis people are not allowed to live here anymore. . . . Tutsis are bad, they are our enemies, and they have to leave." I did not understand what they were talking about, but I was scared. *We know who you are!*

Was I in trouble because my family was friends with the family who was attacked? They were certainly Tutsis, I thought. I did not think they were particularly bad people, but why was their son fighting this morning? I started to have some doubts about them. Over the course of the following days, I learned a lot from these same, menacing children: that Tutsis were a small minority; that Hutus were the majority and backed by soldiers and guns; and, worst of all, that Tutsis were "cockroaches." I did not know then that this stereotype was a nationwide strategy concocted to dehumanize the Tutsi population and eventually make it possible to get rid of them.

I was intrigued by what was happening and needed clarity from my family. Were we safe? It seemed to me we were not. The words "snake" and "cockroach" kept playing in my mind. These were nasty animals people in Rwanda always killed without mercy. Being called these names was clearly not a good thing. I did not ask my parents though, but I spoke instead to Makongo, who worked for my family and lived with us. He was much older than me, probably in his twenties, but I felt very comfortable around him and often confided in him about many things. "We are Hutu, aren't we?" I asked him.

In my mind this was not a question. It was rather a plea that I had hoped would deliver me from the clutches of the prejudice I had just encountered in school. I knew we were good people, who believed in God, went to church every Sunday, and said prayers at the dinner table and before bedtime every evening. Both my parents worked at the hospital, my father as a physician's assistant and my mother as a nurse. They helped a lot of people and were reportedly liked by the local community.

Makongo did not exactly answer my question. Instead, and after a moment of hesitation, he said, "Do not worry, your family is loved around here, and I'm sure nothing will happen to you." If there is something I have always excelled at, even when I was a little boy, it is reading body language. Why did it take him several seconds to formulate his answer? And why did he not keep eye contact while talking to me? My nine-year-old mind could not be fooled. From that moment, I suspected I was a Tutsi. The discovery of my ethnicity left me with a sour taste of fear in my mouth and intensified my feelings of isolation and vulnerability. I felt exposed and stripped of my confidence.

I spent the next couple of days listening for any suspicious movement and watching everything with vigilance. I started paying attention to my parents' reactions, for any hint of fear. I thought I noticed a change in their behavior. They seemed to be whispering every time my siblings and I were around, as if they did not want us to hear. Were they now constantly anxious, or was it simply my imagination? My father, who usually worked long hours, was now home promptly after five. He did not seem as confident as usual. I noticed that families that used to visit us were not coming anymore. I even had the impression that my teachers and my friends at school were no longer friendly. Definitely something was off. Everything was strange.

I began to wonder why my parents had moved to this part of the country the previous year. For several years we had lived in Butare, the capital of the Southern Province and second largest city in the country. It was economically more prosperous, socially more connected, and culturally more integrated. The Belgian rulers had named the city Astrida, in honor of Queen Astrid of Belgium. This historical fact added value to the pride visibly shown by the residents of the region. I knew nothing of the role played by the former colonial power in introducing policies of division between the Hutus and the Tutsis, planting seeds of hatred that would bear poisonous fruit.

The commercial district of Butare was vibrant, throbbing with activity all day long. Its street lights and neon signs had made a lasting impression on me; maybe they represented a powerful connection to a modern world, a sense of belonging to a global society. In comparison with Butare, it felt now as if we were living in some kind of exile, on the margins of society. I could feel it not only in my bones but in the increasing social messages that reinforced my growing sense that we counted for nothing. I started feeling like a foreigner in my own land, and I started to worry about being attacked early in the morning by mad people carrying machetes. I wondered how long we would have to live there, or if we would ever return to Butare.

One evening, at the beginning of summer vacation, my parents came home from work with two other couples. Judging by their animated conversation, they were in a festive mood. Makongo and I were sent to the nearest store to buy a case of Primus, the country's favorite beer. At the bar, people were listening to the radio and speaking so loudly that I could not understand everything. On our way back home, Makongo explained that the country was undergoing "a coup d'état." I did not know what this meant, but apparently it was a big deal for everybody. I would learn later that on July 5, 1973, the military had removed the civilian president, who was accused of dividing the population and inciting ethnic violence. I did not know then that many Tutsi all over the country had their properties confiscated, their houses burned, or their lives taken from them. Many people, including several of my uncles, aunts, and cousins on both sides living around the country, had fled to neighboring countries after being beaten and receiving death threats. The new president was none other than Major General Juvénal Habyarimana, a Hutu from the North of Rwanda, then chief of the army. He promised to end segregation and restore order and harmony among the population during what he called "the Second Republic."

Nobody knew how this new chapter would end. For the moment though, my parents seemed relaxed and happy. I even started hearing that we might head back South. I hoped this was not a rumor.

5

Home

The change of the government quickly brought tranquility in the country. The official message was all about unity, peace, and prosperity. It was a complete reversal of the recent situation where the message was to hunt down people of the Tutsi minority group. People started coming back to our house and apparently having a good time with my parents. These were the same people who had recently avoided us. Surprisingly, it was as though nothing had happened. I, however, was still marked with the scars left by the discovery of the dark side of human nature. Deep inside, I felt my trust in people was not going to be the same.

My parents had indeed requested to move back to our native city of Nyanza in the South; they wanted to be closer to my great grandmother living alone in the surrounding rural area. Miraculously their request was granted by the new administration. One morning that summer of 1973, as we had done many times before, a large truck came before dawn and we packed all our belongings; my parents sat next to the truck driver in the front with my baby sister, Rose; I, my other four siblings, Aimable, Chantal, Julienne, and Jean Paul, then Makongo and our dog, Bobby, climbed in the back of the truck on top of the furniture. We all left the place without looking behind.

The unpaved road was long and bumpy. The truck moved slowly, leaving a cloud of dust and smoke behind us. Often, we crossed military trucks full of armed soldiers. Their features were frightening. After several hours on the road, our truck was stopped by soldiers at a roadblock erected before a large bridge. This was the Nyabarongo River, Makongo explained. The soldiers asked my parents to show their identity cards. Intimidating questions were asked and nervous answers were given. The soldiers took their time, which seemed like an eternity. Eventually, my parents' documents were returned, and we were allowed to proceed. Makongo later explained that the roadblock was to identify and arrest "cockroaches" who might intend to harm the country.

"Sometimes cockroaches are caught and thrown into the river," he had added, with an evident appreciation for the "job" the army was doing. Makongo was someone I usually trusted; I found him kind and reliable in many ways. He was not an educated person, but I often counted on his advice anyway. This time, though, I found his reasoning frightening.

My family settled in our hometown of Nyanza in a modest middle-class neighborhood of civil servants who did not meddle unnecessarily in our life. Our house was of brick walls, red tile roof, and cement floors. It had three small bedrooms, a living room, and a dining room. I shared a bedroom with my two brothers, while my three younger sisters shared the other room. The place was small but I was happy. Across the yard was a large annex that contained the kitchen, a bedroom, and the bathroom. The property was surrounded by a tall and thick cypress hedge, which kept dust from reaching our house. It was in the heart of the town, only a five-minute walk from the commercial district, the school, the church, and the hospital, where my parents worked. I was amazed how everything was in walking distance. I was home now, and safe.

There were seven other similar houses along the street, which made the neighborhood a lively place to live. There was a water tap down the street in front of our house, which we shared with all our neighbors. My brother Aimable and I would take turns helping Makongo keep full the large barrel that my family used to store water. The shared tap was more than the source of our clean water; it was a place of daily rendezvous and fun. I loved the stories and jokes that accompanied our water sourcing routine. They brought the young people of the neighborhood together and made enjoyable an otherwise unpleasant chore.

Gradually I came to love my new environment. The local community in general was very friendly, and there was no indication whatsoever that people cared about ethnicity. Very quickly I recovered from my recent traumatic experience. It seemed unlikely that we would again be subject to intimidation because of our ethnicity. I had not understood why people from the "Tutsi" ethnic group, to which I now knew I belonged, had been threatened. I did not see any difference between us and the Hutu people. I was ready to settle down and enjoy my new life.

Every morning I woke up to the sounds of a neighborhood in effervescence. I could hear people conversing happily, cars roaring, and children playing soccer down the street. They were sounds of life. My brother Aimable and I were having a blast. Aimable was only a year and a half older than I, which made it possible to have the same friends and share the same interests. Soccer was our number-one hobby. We would play for hours down the street with our new friends or in the parking lot of a building behind our house. Aimable and I learned how to make soccer balls from plastic bags, strips of cloth, or dried banana leaves. Eventually I found a brand new latex ball lost inside the cypress hedge behind my house. A ball that could bounce! It was one of the most precious items I had ever owned so far.

On Sundays my parents took us to church. It was a large and imposing structure of stone and bricks that towered above the city on elevated terrain. My father explained that the church was built in 1935. He said he was baptized there when he was a child. There was a gigantic statue planted in front of the church with the inscription "Christ the King." It always gave me a good feeling to be watched over by that statue. We often attended the third morning Mass, and the church was always packed. For me, it was a sign; if the people had faith, that meant they were good people. At the end of the Mass, my parents would stay a while in front of the church, conversing happily with other parents. Occasionally, Aimable and I would sneak behind the church to play soccer.

Two of the children we played with, Abraham and Kalinganire, became our best friends. We shared a passion for soccer and shooting marbles. Abraham's parents were farmers and lived on the outskirts of the town. I would occasionally sneak into his modest straw-thatched house without my parents' knowledge to share a meal; the meal often consisted of "Bugali," a starchy dish made from cassava flour, and beans. It was a modest dish, with no meat, but I enjoyed it. Kalinganire came from the Twa ethnic group, which represented less than 1 percent of the population. It was said they were the first inhabitants of Rwanda before the Hutu and Tutsi arrived, but they were economically disadvantaged. Kalinganire was a friendly, gentle boy who wanted to fit in and belong somewhere. He and the Twa community deserved that. They were deprived and marginalized, but they were in my view among the nicest people I had ever known.

Abraham and Kalinganire helped us discover the beauty of our town. Beyond the imposing church and the dynamic commercial district were the school quarters, which included the Christ-Roi College and the Collège des Humanités Modernes, two very well-known high schools in the country. Down the street was the region's hospital, where my parents worked, while farther north were the administrative quarters, which consisted of the Supreme Court and other lower courts, the Parquet de la République (prosecutor's office), the post office, the town offices, and the police station. There was a beautiful wooded residential area with large colonial houses, where expatriates, justices from the courts, and other officials lived. I dreamed of someday living in a similar house.

On an isolated but beautiful hill was the former king's palace, which was now a museum. I had visited it with my parents and was amazed by its size and beauty. It occasionally hosted cultural events, where local and national troops performed dances, particularly "Intore"—the dance of heroes, and drums. The museum seemed deserted. It was said that the Rwandan government did not want to publicize anything that was related to the era of the kingdom. From the hill you could see the soccer stadium, home of the beloved local team, Rayon Sport. The team was like the glue that held the community together. Whenever there was a game, all activities in the town and the surrounding areas were put on hold. Every resident was a fan—from the mayor to the farmer to the little boy in elementary school. On game days, fans packed the stadium and chanted in unison. They celebrated when the team won and grieved together when it lost. In any case they were united by the spirit of solidarity.

I found the town lively and exciting, but it was the countryside that I loved the most. Now that my family lived closer to my great-grandmother, I got to see her as often as opportunities allowed. She lived on the family farmland, about ten kilometers from the city. She was the only grandparent I knew. Nobody knew exactly how old she was. In my estimate she was between ninety and one hundred years old. I remember her skin was so winkled that my siblings and I always intently stared at her forehead and soft cheeks, amazed by the natural transformation that comes with time. But her mind was as sharp as that of a young woman. People were always astonished by her ability to take care of the property and the livestock. She knew every cow by name (yes, cows in Rwanda have names), and she knew when the crops would be ready for harvest.

My family bought most of our food at the farmers' market in our town, but we would get some from our farmland as well. My parents would send my brother Aimable, Makongo, and me to get milk, vegetables, and fruit and bring my great-grandmother money for the laborers. The farmland was reachable by road, but transportation was too expensive for such a short distance. We would walk a couple of hours through hills and valleys, occasionally stopping at a rural fountain to drink water and refresh our faces.

I got to discover the splendid beauty of the countryside. The green land was a natural paradise, where no polluting engine had ever ventured. The air we inhaled was of exquisite purity and was perfumed with the pleasant scents of nature brought by the soft breeze blowing through eucalyptus trees scattered over the green hills. One could wonder how this landscape came to be. Hills succeeded hills in a perfect undulation, separated by flat valleys meandering indefinitely, with small streams of fresh and clear water running through them. It could only be the work of the creator. No wonder that Rwandans believed in God.

We would often pass peasants working methodically the terraced hillsides; they would eventually pause and greet us with kind words, then resume their work. Farther down in the valleys, we could see cows and sheep attended by young shepherds carrying long sticks.

Our farmland extended from the top of a hill called Ngorongari ("large castle") to the valley. My father had built on the property a small house with cement floors and a tile roof, easily accessible from the main road. It was surrounded by different sorts of plantations, which included banana trees, beans, sweet potatoes, corn, and sorghum. There were fruit trees, particularly avocado, papaya, and guava trees planted all around the property. I loved spending time there, among these plants. They were my silent companions. My favorite spot was the lower part of the farmland, in the valley, at the edge of the property. The valley was flat and the soft grass was green. I loved to lie down and look at the open blue sky. The place was pure, extremely calm, and beautiful. It was a place where maybe nobody had ever set foot before. It conveyed a feeling of peace and serenity—a feeling of happiness and fullness of life. I would stay there for hours, until sunset.

I loved evenings on the farmland. The daylight always faded beautifully, with the sun displaying softly its golden rays in the horizon and disappearing gracefully behind the remote hills. Dusk came with the sounds of nature; the croaking of frogs and the creaking of crickets produced dramatic yet soothing tones that accompanied the sleeping valleys. At this soundtrack shepherds ushered the cattle up the hill to their stables in the backyard of the farmhouse. It was a sign for my brother, Makongo, and me to go back home, reversing the route taken earlier through the same hills and valleys, walking fast against a gentle breeze, under a moonlit sky. Peace was all around us.

I did not know then that the quietude we had on that "land of a thousand hills" was only on the surface. Deep under were layers of conflict and hatred, laid by a history of political divisions. I began seeing some of the signs when school started in the fall. I was entering fifth grade.

6

Rwanda: The Country of "Cold" Peace

School started with a routine that always made me anxious. Our teacher ordered Tutsi children to stand up every morning. I always rose slowly, frightened. A few other children in the classroom did the same, while the rest of the students stared, feeling sorry for us. I remember I always got a fluttery feeling in the stomach every time the teacher started the ethnic roll call. We remained standing for a brief moment, but it was the most terrifying experience of my school time. My friend Abraham was among those who remained seated. He was a Hutu. That was all right; he was always nice to me, and we remained friends.

"You can sit down now," the teacher always said, putting down his list. He never asked us for anything, and I did not exactly understand the reason for this bizarre ritual. I later learned my teacher was not the only one to perform this morning ethnic roll call; other teachers did the same. For some time, I was confused. These teachers were friendly and seemed to be good people. Most attended Mass every Sunday with their families, and many were catechists who took part in various activities of the church. I played soccer with their children and sometimes went to their homes. I never saw any antipathy toward me. So why did they inflict a traumatic experience on every school day?

Eventually I heard that the roll call was something they had to do, not a practice of their choosing. It was as though they were executing orders coming from invisible powers, which maintained a state of fear and mistrust in the community. Social anxiety was perceptible. A closer look at people's behavior revealed a subtle, concealed unease of being open and forthcoming about anything. In general, fear was a factor that drove people's behavior. I could see it in people around me: teachers, family friends, neighbors, and people in the street. People were fearful of authority figures and of officers in the army, who, for most part, were native of the president's region in the North; they had been sent to the region to enforce the president's authoritarian policies. People also feared members of the intelligence services, who often abused their power and intimidated the community.

By the time I went to high school, I had learned more about Rwanda's history and the factors that had fostered ethnic division and led to a climate of suspicion and distrust among people. It was no secret that the fear that hung over people's heads was deliberately maintained by the government.

My parents never talked about the troubles of the past, probably not wanting to frighten their children. But I heard they had lived through some terrifying moments. Just a few weeks before I was born, most Tutsi men living in the northern city of Ruhengeri, where my parents worked at the local hospital, were jailed and some were coldly executed. My father was arrested as well and briefly jailed, but he was released unhurt. Nurses and medical personnel were needed and were therefore spared. My mother proved to be particularly helpful aiding local women, including military wives, deliver their babies. The house my parents rented was burned down, as it was owned by a Tutsi. Thankfully someone had warned them.

All of my mother's direct relatives, however, were threatened and forced into exile. My grandfather, Romuald Sebutimbiri, fled to the neighboring country of Burundi with his siblings and all his sons and daughters. They left their home and their land in Nyaruguru, a district in southeastern Rwanda not far from Kibeho, a small town that later became a pilgrimage for Catholics after an apparition of the Blessed Mother. In the northwestern region of Burundi, where they settled down, they acquired refugee status, not realizing it was to become their identity for decades to come.

I grew up with that void, the feeling that I had been deprived of the joy of being surrounded by a large family, simply because they were in exile and couldn't cross the border. I always heard good things about my relatives, particularly my maternal grandfather, who was said to be a man of great character, known for high moral qualities and a strong faith in God. I longed to meet him some day, and all the other people connected to me by blood.

The opportunity presented itself in the summer of 1979 when my aunt Julie came to visit us from Burundi. She was the second youngest of my mother's siblings. I loved her at first sight. She was like a big sister to me. She told us stories about life in Burundi and brought pictures of the family members we had never met. One picture was of my grandfather surrounded by his entire family. Another was of my uncle Hermenegilde, pastor of a Catholic parish in the Burundian capital. Other pictures showed several of my cousins. I was amazed how many relatives I had. Although they were in exile, they were well and alive.

When Julie suggested that my sister Chantal and I go with her to visit family members in Burundi, I did not hide my excitement. But soon I got worried when my parents started going through the details of our trip. We did not have travel documents and we couldn't get any. It was quite impossible for Tutsis to be issued passports. The plan was to have my uncle Sebuturumba, a farmer who was familiar with the region, go along with us up to the Akanyaru River, which separates the two countries, and then proceed by foot through the mountains in northern Burundi. My sister and I were asked not to tell the neighbors about the trip. Visiting refugees abroad was forbidden. My parents could be reported to local authorities and jailed.

One morning that summer, Julie, my uncle, Chantal, and I left our house before dawn and took public transportation to the city of Butare, and from there we rode in the back of a pickup truck that took us to a rural commercial center close to the border with Burundi. We followed a narrow path through the woods and banana plantations in the hills, then descended toward the Akanyaru River. It was larger than I had imagined. There were a few men waiting to take passengers on the other side. My uncle negotiated the tariff and an agreement was quickly reached. One of the men took the money, then pulled a small wooden boat from nowhere and pushed it into the water. The crossing took less than ten minutes but it felt like an eternity. The boat was too low and felt unstable under our weight and our bags. I did not know how to swim and prayed the boat would not capsize. I was shaken when we landed on the other side. We waved my uncle goodbye and started our ascent up a steep hill that towered over the river. We were now in foreign territory.

We had walked about twenty minutes through plantations when peasants working the field on the side of a hill told us there was an ambush ahead. *"Babateze"* ("you have been ambushed"), they warned us. The peasants' helpless expression signaled there was nothing they could do. We literally froze. Suddenly we heard yells echoing from the top of the hill; they were like chilling, primal screams of antelope hunters. We ran for our lives down the hill. We heard our assailants running behind us and we ran faster. We all stumbled and fell. Our bodies rolled down the hill and came to rest in a coffee plantation. My knee was hurting, and I found that it was injured. In the process Julie lost her bag and my brand-new sweater, which she was carrying for me. This must have slowed down the aggressors, as they may have abandoned their pursuit to go after the bag and the sweater. But we did not stop running until we were certain no one was chasing us anymore. "These were just thieves," Julie said, to reassure us as we proceeded in the Burundian countryside. I was not reassured. Had it been possible, I would have returned home.

We reached a small rural commercial center and waited hours for transportation. Finally, a pickup truck showed up, and several people jumped in the back. The truck was so full I was afraid I was going to suffocate. We rode on a dusty road to the city of Ngozi in northern Burundi, and then from there took an overcrowded minibus to the Burundian capital, Bujumbura, where we arrived late at night. It was hard to believe that a distance of two hundred kilometers or less took a whole day to cover. But, as I would learn later, the political tensions between Rwanda and Burundi did not make it easy for people to travel freely. While the government and the army in Rwanda were led by Hutu, power in Burundi was in the hands of Tutsi. At the middle of the tense relationships was the problem of refugees, each country fearing destabilization by its citizens who sought refuge in the other country.

My uncle Hermenegilde, a tall priest with a deep voice, hosted us at his parish for the night and drove us the following morning to the northwestern region of Burundi where the rest of the family lived. We arrived at my grandfather's house in the afternoon. It was a small squared mud house covered with corrugated metal roofing sheets. Similar houses were aligned along the parallel streets of that flat rural land that Rwandan refugees were given by the government of Burundi to share. The inside of the house was modest but clean and organized.

My grandfather was sitting in a chair in the small living room. A picture of him hung on the wall behind him. He was wearing a spotless, white traditional costume with well-polished black shoes at his feet. The rosary around his neck indicated he was still loyal to his Catholic faith. A statue of the Virgin Mary that stood in a corner transmitted the same message. It was an almost exact replica of the statue that my mother kept in the living room back home. It was as though the Mother of Jesus was the link between a father and a daughter separated by unfortunate destiny.

My grandfather's lean frame revealed he had been healthy and strong. His face was straight with a long nose and strong chin, prolonged by a neatly trimmed white goatee that gave him a very distinguished look. I could see everyone in the house treated him with respect. He took me by the shoulders and looked at me for a long moment; his gaze was kind and soothing. A slight smile lit up his face as he gave me a long embrace. When I looked at him again though, the look in his eyes had assumed a sad expression, subtly revealing the deep pain embedded in his heart.

During the three-week period I spent in Burundi, all the relatives I met, particularly the elders, seemed resigned to a state of despair. They all put on a dignified look but couldn't hide their emotional hardship. My teenage mind couldn't then grasp the depth of their hopelessness. I came to understand later that they had been driven to the bottom of a society that never embraced them totally. They had long realized they might not get a chance to change their refugee status, be reunited with family members still in Rwanda, see the land that had been their home for most of their lives, and dare to dream again.

I left Burundi with a mixed feeling of pride and sadness. I was grateful for having met so many family members, most of whom were noble people of faith and dignity. I was proud to be their grandson or nephew or cousin. At the same time, I wondered if we would ever have a chance to be the one, strong family I longed to have.

The letters and pictures I brought back home put a smile on my mother's lips; they brought tears too. My mother did not ask questions nor did she make comments. I thought I perceived in her expression the same resignation and sense of helplessness I saw in our relatives on the other side of the border. She knew the chances of seeing her father and siblings again under the dictatorial regime presiding over our country were close to none.

Indeed, Rwanda had become an authoritarian state. The country's president, Juvénal Habyarimana, had installed a vertical administrative structure under his complete supervision and created a strong intelligence apparatus. He appointed all regional leaders, often chosen from his loyal entourage. The country was divided into prefectures, communes, sectors, and cells. This centralized granular structure allowed him to take control of the information sent to or coming from the lowest levels of the administration. The structure in place allowed him to follow the movements of individuals, and especially to monitor any sign of refugees trying to return. Consequently, no one inside Rwanda dared openly to maintain contact with their families in exile.

Every Rwandan was required to belong to a cell and to give a financial contribution to the Mouvement Révolutionaire National pour le Développement (MRND), the only political party allowed and to which every citizen belonged. Every week, all workers from the public and private sector participated in mandatory gatherings to praise President Habyarimana and the MRND—often just referred to as "the movement." These political and brainwashing rituals were conducted by the most zealous members of the party, many of whom were from the president's native region. They shouted out slogans, praising "the movement" and calling the president the "Father of the Nation." The audience repeated after them. Under rhythmic songs composed for the occasion, they shook their bodies, raised their hands, turned, twisted, bent and rose in a frenzy of movements, and the audience did the same. Everybody knew this was absurd, but no one dared to protest. The media was controlled 100 percent by the government and played its expected role in singing the praises of the Father of the Nation. Through mass media, propaganda, praise, and silence, Rwandans created a cult of personality. President Habyarimana was worshiped like a god and his unique party followed like a religion. In each of the country's three elections, he was elected with 99 percent of the votes. The average Rwandan was still poor, and people around the country were hurting; but they surrendered to the propaganda machine and chose to believe that Habyarimana was their only salvation. The international community, including the Vatican, played along, praising the president as the guarantor of the country's stability.

By the time I finished college in the mid-1980s and started my career in Kigali, Rwanda was portrayed on the international stage as a beacon of peace. The reality, however, was that the country's serenity was built upon sand. The peace that Rwandan authorities were advertising was only a mirage, and the world was to learn soon that this was not peace, but the absence of war.

7

The Rising of the Magma

The number of Rwandan refugees living in foreign countries, mostly in neighboring states but also in Europe and North America, had grown to nearly half a million people in the late 1980s. It was rumored that they wanted to return to Rwanda, but President Habyarimana refused to let them in, arguing that Rwanda was already overcrowded and couldn't accommodate more people.

That angered the refugees. Most of them were born in exile, were young, and had a great desire to see their country. Some of the members of the Rwandan diaspora started calling for a united front against Habyarimana, vowing, one day, to secure the repatriation of all refugees.

My grandfather did not live to see that day. He died in exile in 1989. We mourned his death in silence and in secret. A year later, in the summer of 1990, I was able to travel to Burundi again with my mother, on the occasion of the first anniversary of my grandfather's passing. This time we had passports, which I obtained through a former high school classmate, a moderate Hutu who was now the head of Immigration Services.

We put flowers on the grave and said prayers. A picture of my grandfather was on display against the headstone. His face showed the same calmness, the same distinctive and dignified look I had seen a decade ago. My mother took time to say goodbye to a father she had last seen thirty years before, when she was only twenty. The Rwandan refugee community and all the relatives in exile were there around her. It was a bittersweet moment of sorrow and reunion.

This time, surprisingly, I did not see in the refugees' eyes the same hopelessness and resignation I had seen a decade ago. Instead I saw something different—*anger and defiance*. The same young men with whom I had played and laughed during my last visit now adopted a tough, politically oriented language that expressed aversion to the Rwandan government. They sang patriotic songs with a hint of resentment and hostility. Obviously, something was in the air, but I did not know what.

On October 1, 1990, I was traveling on a business mission from North Africa to Geneva, Switzerland, with a consultant from Egypt working for the International Trade Center (ITC), a Swiss-based organization that had sponsored my trip. In transit at Charles de Gaulle Airport in Paris, Mustafa, the Egyptian, casually pointed to a TV screen and told me Rwanda was in the news. I approached to hear what was being reported. The news hit me like a ton of bricks. The French channel was reporting that Rwanda had been attacked from its northern border with Uganda by a group called the Rwandan Patriotic Front, or RPF.

I was scheduled to return to Rwanda that same week, but my sponsors at ITC kindly suggested that I delay my return by a month. The media reported that during the night of October 4, gunshots were heard in the Rwandan capital. By the morning, the Rwandan army and police had rounded up thousands of Tutsi civilians, most of them civil servants and businessmen, and thrown them in various jails around the city, accusing them of being agents or sympathizers of the RPF. It would soon be known that President Habyarimana had staged the overnight gunshots, literally taking hostage Tutsi civilians as a warning to the RPF fighters, and inciting his base to mistrust the Tutsi population.

Every day I called my house from Geneva to inquire on the safety of my roommates. I lived with Joseph Hategekimana, my best friend from high school and college, who worked now at the ministry of planning, and my cousin Philippe Sengoga, a high school math teacher. They were both Tutsi and obviously scared, but they were safe. Possibly they avoided being rounded up and jailed because we were new in the neighborhood. We lived in a small house located on Kayuku Street in the Kiyovu residential area, relatively close to the secondary presidential residence. The streets in Kiyovu were patrolled by presidential guards, known for their aggressive behavior. But, apparently, they did not notice that there were Tutsi living less than half a mile away. We had rarely met our neighbors, and no one pointed a finger at our house.

When I returned to Rwanda a month later, I saw a completely changed country. There were roadblocks in the streets, and no one could pass without showing an identity card. People would go home early. Thousands of Tutsi civilians had been jailed, and it was reported that some had been killed. At work, I noticed many colleagues stopped talking to me. These were mostly natives of the North, where the president came from. Surprisingly though, even some of my closest acquaintances kept their distance. It was stunning how people's reactions were now pure vitriol. Every morning, people would gather in small groups in the courtyards of their office buildings or at the corner of a street to exchange the latest news. There were more rumors than ever, and suspicion was in the air.

In the weeks and months that followed the attack, the Rwandan government adopted extreme measures to deal with what it incessantly called "cockroaches" or "snakes." They saw us as a "social problem" that needed elimination, and they were ready to step on us at any moment.

Hutu extremists initiated an unprecedented anti-Tutsi campaign. They revived stereotypes from the 1960s, portraying the Tutsis as malignant individuals who stole the country from its "legitimate" Hutu owners. They fostered fear by saying the Tutsis wanted to dominate and exploit the Hutu majority and take away their rights. I never understood this line of thinking, since the majority of Tutsi were some of the poorest people in the country. On the other hand, Hutus largely dominated the government, the economy, and the army.

Truthfully, while the regime was advancing a policy of segregation, most ordinary Hutus had no real aversion toward the Tutsis. Before the war, my Hutu friends had never shown me any sign of antipathy. The racial antagonisms were politically initiated, propagated, and orchestrated. The propagandists wanted to scare the Hutu population and bring them to the point of such fear and terror that they would need to rise up and "defend" themselves. It was a clever, if evil, strategy. In the name of self-defense, murder was being legitimized. Men started sending their wives and children to neighboring countries, fearing for their safety. Many people also started to withdraw their little savings, preparing, if necessary, to leave the country. I too started keeping some cash with me. Just in case.

Various organizations demanded accountability from the government. Human rights groups arose to pressure the government. I began participating in one of the newly formed human rights associations, called Kanyarwanda, which advocated for social justice and peace among all Rwandans, regardless of their ethnic groups. Taking a stand against the Habyarimana regime was dangerous, but I needed to do something. I wanted to play a part in the movement of change. These different human rights groups pushed the international community to create a human rights commission for Rwanda. The commission found evidence that President Habyarimana and his entourage had deliberately sanctioned the massacre of the Tutsi in the northwestern region between 1990 and 1993. Many donor nations, which the government relied on heavily for development assistance, demanded accountability for these abuses and threatened to cut back on their financial assistance.

In the face of this international pressure, the Habyarimana regime reluctantly agreed to accept power-sharing principles and to enter into negotiations with the opposition and the RPF. Political parties inside the country formed a transitional government, which included both Tutsis and moderate Hutu opposition leaders. With the mediation of the Tanzanian government and the Organization of African Unity (OAU), the Rwandan government reluctantly signed a cease-fire and a peace agreement with the Rwandan Patriotic Front in August 1993.

The violence temporarily stopped, but the underlying tensions remained. Peace required more than the absence of war, for ethnic hatred still festered in the hearts of many. Nevertheless, the international community had helped Rwanda take a step forward. In October 1993, the UN Security Council decided to establish an international force, the United Nations Assistance Mission for Rwanda (UNAMIR), to help implement the peace agreement and support the establishment of a broad-based government. The first contingents of UN troops were offered by Belgium and Bangladesh; they arrived in Rwanda in December 1993, and started to patrol the streets of Kigali. As part of the peace arrangement, the RPF sent to Kigali leaders designated to be members of the broad-based government along with six hundred of its troops.

With the arrival of the UN contingent and RPF troops in Rwanda, many Rwandans felt hopeful. I certainly did. People who had sent their families abroad even started bringing them back. Despite the hateful propaganda of Hutu extremists, people in general did not foresee major catastrophic events. Or maybe, having lived on the edge for so long, we were just too eager to relax our guard.

We saw militiamen as illegal gangs that could not have a lasting hold on people's lives. Whenever we heard them singing *"Tuzabatsembatsemba"* ("we will massacre you"), we did not take it seriously. We interpreted their songs more like political slogans, simply meant to instill fear among opponents of the Habyarimana regime. What we did not realize, however, was that the militia's message was making its way into many heads, preparing a bomb that was ready to detonate. For three years now, we had known we were living on a land of dynamite, but we had all hoped its fuse would never be lit. We were wrong.

PART II

Death

The swamp outside of Ntarama, where thousands died.

8

A Country on Dynamite

On the morning of April 7, 1994, following the death of President Habyarimana, the news on national radio turned my blood cold. A communiqué from the Rwandan authorities ordered everybody to stay home. I immediately knew this development was not good. Cautiously, I locked all the doors and closed the curtains. I was not sure what difference barricading myself inside the house was going to make, but it felt safer. The radio stations were broadcasting somber classical music, occasionally interrupted by communiqués from the military command. The tone of the hosts on the infamous RTLM radio, now known as the voice of the extremists, was more violent than usual. They were openly calling for the extermination of "cockroaches," which meant us. I checked Radio France International and the BBC. Both stations were delivering disturbing news and talking about evacuating European citizens working in Rwanda.

Later in the evening, the media announced that Rwandan soldiers had killed Agathe Uwilingiyimana, the prime minister of Rwanda, at her residence. This was especially frightening news, a sure sign that Rwanda was headed toward chaos. The prime minister was a brave woman, regarded as one of the most moderate Hutu politicians in the country. Her assassination certainly meant the country had fallen into the hands of the extremists. Later, it was reported that the same Rwandan soldiers had killed ten Belgian members of the UN peacekeeping mission, serving as her security detail. The prime minister's residence was less than two miles away; these killings were happening in my neighborhood. Now I started to panic. Surely it was only a matter of time before

49

the killers were going to reach my house. I did not know then that Belgium was about to withdraw all its troops from Rwanda and that the UN Security Council was about to vote unanimously to reduce the number of UN soldiers from 2,500 to only 250 men, leaving us at the mercy of extremists.

A phone call from one of my college friends, Gustave Nyoni, added to the panic. He told me soldiers of the presidential guard had just killed one of my neighbors, Jean Bosco Gahigi, an employee of the National Bank, whose house on Kamuzinzi Street could be seen from my backyard. Gustave also said his neighborhood was under attack, and he feared for his life.

I desperately needed to contact my fiancée. I called her landlord and thankfully he reached Christine. At first she did not sound too scared, which surprised me. But as we talked, I felt a hint of worry in her voice. Maybe the gravity of my tone added to her concern. We spoke briefly and exchanged survival tips, hoping they would not be needed.

Christine reminded me that her boss, a Belgian named Jean Marie Sammin, had advised us a few weeks earlier to go to the "Swiss Village," where all expatriates and personnel working for projects funded by the Swiss government would assemble for safety in case of trouble. Employees of European-funded projects had been asked to provide their contact information for protection or evacuation if necessary. The Swiss Village, a complex of apartments temporarily housing Swiss personnel in Rwanda, was not far from my house. It gave me some peace of mind that Christine's boss cared for our safety; but the security situation was still very precarious, and it remained an open question if we would get out of this alive.

Later that day I called my parents. (Thank God they had a phone, which was recently installed.) My father answered and told me the family was safe and that there was no violence in our hometown. I was somewhat relieved. Maybe the crazed killers would not reach the South. Despite his assurance, I could still sense anxiety in his voice. He had lived through an earlier wave of massacres and knew the destructive capacities of the regime. And right now, five of his children were caught in the middle of the chaos in the capital.

Just three days ago, I had brought my younger brother Regis and younger sister Rose to spend their school break in Kigali, helping my sister Chantal with her two-month-old son. Christine and I had picked them up at my parents' house in Nyanza while driving from the southern city of Butare.

I told my father we were fine, although I was not sure this was true.

I thought, as well, of two mothers to whom we had given a ride from Butare to Kigali. One of them was my mother's cousin, Cecile Sebalinda, who left her two young children behind with her parents. The children wouldn't let her leave, and she had to hide from them and sneak into our car from the backyard. The other woman left her daughter with her older sibling, a nun of the Little Sisters of Jesus. I remembered how both women wept during the trip to Kigali. Now I just hoped they would soon be reunited with their children.

I was now, however, more concerned about Christine's family living in the southeastern region of Bugesera. That region, known for its large Tutsi population, had been subjected to many of the worst massacres in the past. It was widely known that Tutsis living in Bugesera bore the highest risk. I could only pray that the current turmoil was concentrated in the capital.

Over the next two days, however, Rwanda continued the descent into a spiral of violence. Although we received news about a transitional government, some international radio stations began reporting news about large-scale massacres. The formation of a new government was a good thing, I thought; at least someone was in charge. But why did the new president not talk to the nation and order a stop to the massacres? Obviously, something was wrong. I kept listening to the national news, hoping to hear a message of peace. But that message never came.

The national radio also started releasing official communiqués, calling government employees by name to return to work. I was startled when I heard my name on the radio, among other people's names. I literally froze; what was I supposed to do? Something told me I should not leave my home. It was too dangerous out there. I did not know then that those who responded did not make it to their offices; one of the victims, called Nyemazi, was a well-known government employee. When he showed up for work at the ministry of finance, where he worked, he was executed on the spot. I feared that sooner or later, someone would figure out where I lived and get me into trouble.

I called a friend for help. Thomas Mbateye was a coworker and a true friend I trusted. He and his wife were good people, very much involved in faith-based activities at the St. Michel Cathedral, where we both attended Mass. I regularly visited his family two streets away from my house. They were Hutu, but I never looked at them in terms of ethnicity. Mbateye happened to be an acquaintance—and neighbor—of General Augustin Ndindiriyimana, then chief of staff of the *Gendarmerie Nationale,* the National Police. Unfortunately, Mbateye had not seen his powerful neighbor for days; there was nothing he could do, and he did not feel safe himself, he told me. My hopes vanished and my anxiety doubled. I was on my own.

9

The Smell of Death

The morning of April 10 was bright and beautiful. For the first time in four days, I had slept through the night. With the exception of the sound of occasional gunshots in the distance, everything around me was quiet. But I doubted peace had returned. It felt more like the calm before the storm. I knew I needed to get out this place—but I had no idea how to get to Christine. Streets were barricaded with roadblocks. I needed to come up with a plan. When I called, her landlord picked up the phone. He was not at all happy to hear from me. "Do you realize that you are putting all of us at risk?" he shouted. "Leave her alone!" I wondered if something had happened.

But I soon realized he was just scared. I did not blame him. The risk was real; there were rumors on the radio that "cockroaches" had infiltrated people's homes in the city; the radio was calling for a thorough search of all residences. Reluctantly, he called Christine to the phone, and a few minutes later I heard her voice. We had barely started our conversation when I heard commotion in the background. The landlord and his wife sounded agitated. Christine's next words, uttered with her voice trembling and articulated in a faint whisper, filled me with terror: "They are here; they are surrounding the house."

I could sense fear in her voice; fear as I had never felt it before. She was whispering, her voice trembling. Her words through the phone line conveyed a deep sense of despair and panic that sent a chill down my spine. I knew who "they" were: the killers. In my mind I could picture them, advancing quietly and confidently, like hunters closing in on their prey, knowing it had no chance of escape.

What I had feared was happening, and there was nothing I could do. I blamed myself for not having left this place when I had the chance, taking my fiancée with me to safety. But who knew life in Kigali was going to get so bad and deteriorate so quickly? Now it was too late. I felt powerless. The army and the Interahamwe militia had closed streets to traffic, putting roadblocks everywhere. The city was in a state of chaos, held hostage by armed soldiers and merciless militiamen who killed ruthlessly. They were in the first stage of a total ethnic cleansing.

I was about to say something to reassure my fiancée, but what words would help at a moment like this? And then I heard a shot, followed by a scream; then the phone line went dead. I screamed in rage. Feeling totally helpless, I dropped to my knees and began to pray, begging God for one thing and one thing only: a miracle.

Late morning, the roaring sound of an approaching vehicle made me jump to my feet. I cautiously peered through a closed curtain to see what was happening. What I saw warmed my heart and began to bring me back to life. Two soldiers had just jumped from their military jeep and started marching toward my house. As the driver maneuvered into a strategic position, a half dozen other soldiers surrounded the property; these were European soldiers. Suddenly I had hope. "Finally, the saviors have arrived," I thought to myself.

As the soldiers marched toward my home, I thanked God for answering my prayers and being my shield. At that moment, their army combat uniforms, red berets, and state-of-the-art machine guns symbolized the best use of power, namely, the power to protect the innocent from harm. I felt lucky I lived on a civilized planet, and there were people who valued human beings for their intrinsic worth, regardless of their ethnic status. But how did they find us? Through technology? Or word of mouth? Or perhaps Christine's boss?

I raced to the front door, yanked it wide, and ran toward the soldiers with a big smile on my face. The lead commander approached slowly, adopting a ready-to-shoot position. He showed no emotion. He asked in French if I knew where a certain lady named Corinne lived. I assumed these were French troops. His words struck me like a thunderclap. I immediately understood they had not come for me. I said I did not know her. In a fraction of a second, the soldiers left my property, jumped in their jeep, and sped off. It was as though they had only existed in my dream.

Deeply disappointed, I stood there for a moment, refusing to admit that my hope had just vanished. It was a gorgeous morning, yet the events did not seem to match the beauty of the day. From the street above, I heard voices; probably some of the presidential guards who were patrolling the streets of the Kiyovu residential area. I literally ran back to my house, hoping I had not been seen.

Once again, I slammed the front door and locked it behind me. How naïvely I had trusted! What a fool I had become! How could I think for a moment that the Western troops had come for us? People around the world are killed every day, but most of the time no one comes to their rescue. Why would French troops care about me? How could I be so incautious? And I had just exposed myself and my household to danger by going outside and speaking to these Western soldiers! My entire body felt the impact of this realization: foreigners were being evacuated. It was not a good sign.

But still I refused to abandon hope. Sooner or later I would get out of this house. I went to my bedroom, grabbed my passport, and put it in my shirt pocket. I removed my national ID card and hid it in my socks. I first contemplated destroying my ID, which identified my ethnic group, but then opted for keeping it. I knew this could be a fatal decision, but it was riskier not to have it. Then I hid all the money I had in any part of my clothing, including in my socks. Altogether I had saved 840 US dollars in cash, put aside for emergencies, and 13,000 Rwandan francs for my daily needs.

At this time I was startled by a knock on my bedroom door. It was Sophanie, who worked for us. "There are soldiers in the backyard," he whispered.

I knew at once that these must be presidential guards—the only soldiers stationed in our neighborhood, which was close to the second presidential residence. They had a reputation for fierceness and cruelty. I tried to keep a brave face, but I too was scared. This could be the end. I closed my bedroom door and raced to the window. Carefully, I peered from the side of the curtain and looked out in the backyard. There I saw them: two Rwandan soldiers moving toward the back door. Their steps were slow and measured. They wore chains of munitions all around their torsos. The tips of their guns had sharp, piercing bayonets.

My first impulse was to hide. Desperately, I slid under the bed, only to realize immediately how foolish this was. The soldiers surely knew I was in the house. In all likelihood they had seen me talking to the foreign soldiers and watched me go back inside. I knew they would search every corner of the house until they found me, and under the bed was an obvious place to look. Probably they would interpret my hiding as an admission of "guilt."

With no other good plan, I walked to the living room and joined my sister and cousins. All of us were shaking. Philippe was breathing heavily. "Let's behave naturally," he said, "as if we are not afraid." That was a good plan. We needed to hide our terror and put up an appearance of normalcy. I sat on the couch, closed my eyes, and said a prayer. Did I look normal? I had never felt so terrified in my life.

Outside, the soldiers were taking their time. Then it happened. A bang on the backdoor pulled all of us back to reality. A loud, menacing voice ordered us to open up. Sophanie looked at me, as if asking my permission. With my nod, he opened the door. Two soldiers rushed in. For a second, I thought they were going to shoot us, but did not. Not now, not yet. Instead, they ordered everybody to go outside. At that same moment, my phone rang. One of the soldiers lifted the receiver and listened, without saying a word. It was my father. I could hear him calling my name.

'Bosco, is it you?" he was asking.

"Speaking," responded the soldier.

"Who are you?" my father asked. "You do not sound like Bosco."

They were the last words I heard my father speak. Immediately, the soldier hung up and cut off the phone line with his bayonet. Then he pushed me outside through the kitchen door. I was shaking. I knew it was over.

There was a third soldier outside. He was a short and bulky man with a pistol instead of a long gun. Probably he was the commander of the team. The three men looked furious. Their faces were merciless; their breath smelled of alcohol and tobacco. My sister Julienne, my cousins Philippe and Murekatete, and Sophanie were also ordered to join me outside. The bulky man ordered us to sit down in the backyard, our backs against the cement wall of the house. We all obeyed without hesitation.

"Show your ID cards," the man shouted. I immediately understood what he was after. He was not interested in our identity, but our ethnicity. I was about to pull my ID from my sock when something told me not to. Instead, I removed my passport from my shirt pocket and handed it to him.

"You do not have an ID card?" the soldier asked, in an accusatory tone. I knew the risk of not having an ID card, but I did my best to explain that I had recently lost it and had ordered a new one.

"They said a new card takes up to four weeks," I said, with as much conviction as I could muster, "and they suggested that I use my passport instead."

The soldier considered this answer for a second and then put all the documents he had collected into his jacket pocket.

Philippe and I exchanged glances. I could tell we were both thinking about the same thing: running for our lives. I shook my head; it was much too risky. No one could venture in the streets without identification documents. It would mean certain death. Besides, even if we could get away without any problem, the rest of the group would probably not survive.

It was now early afternoon. I felt exhausted. We had been sitting on the ground in the backyard for a long time, under an ardent sun. The soldiers grouped a few feet away and talked in low voices. I sensed they were arguing about whether to shoot us now or later. I couldn't believe this was real.

Suddenly, there was a noise—someone was running. Philippe heard it first. He opened his mouth to say something but was interrupted by the sound of gunfire. We all plunged to the ground but remained silent. The soldiers shouted something to our group and ran after the fugitive. I looked around to check who was missing. It was my cousin Murekatete. When I saw the soldiers return, I knew it was over for her. The commander stepped forward and told us: "Stay where you are. We will be back in a few minutes. If anybody else tries to run, you will all be executed." Then, they took off.

We remained seated on the ground, immobile and silent. We all wanted to get up and run but lacked both the courage and the strength. In any case, running was certainly not a good option. Getting caught would mean an immediate and violent death. And besides, we had nowhere to go; they would certainly find us. The streets were patrolled by the presidential guards, and the whole area was surrounded by bloodthirsty, Tutsi-hunting militiamen. We had no security and no protection; we were totally helpless.

My mind began to race, searching anywhere for an option, but there seemed to be none. Looking over at my cousin and my sister, I saw fear and despair in their eyes. They seemed to look to me for guidance. I had never felt so powerless. And I was angry: at the situation, at the world, at myself. Again I asked myself, why had I not fled this country while it was still possible? Sister Teya's fears had come to pass. Now, here I was, sitting in the dirt, watched closely by these mad soldiers who had become agents of death and could at any moment eliminate me and my relatives. I had given up praying, not sure what God could really do at this point. I did not see his strength; I did not feel any hope. Maybe evil was stronger than good.

10

Angels of Life

Was this the tranquil and beautiful country in which I had spent my entire life? Politics aside, Rwandans were fundamentally good people; this I believed. I remembered how, when I was a child, our neighbors and other people in my hometown of Nyanza, many of them Hutu, were good to my family. Almost all people I knew were Christians, mostly Catholics, and their cultural ties to the church and its teachings were powerful. Of course, as I had to admit, there had always been radical individuals with extreme political views. But the vast majority of people I encountered were good, decent human beings. Over many years, I came to know them and their families. I attended their weddings and their children's sacraments. I cried with them at funerals. We shared meals, laughter, and precious memories. Those memories were a bright light in my soul that I hoped would keep shining. But for now it seemed as if the wrong side of heaven had taken over.

As I sat on the ground, searching my mind for any solution, I suddenly had an idea. I thought of Therese, my neighbor. After all, she had called me to share the news about the president's death. I had no doubt she was well intentioned. Also, in past months, she had invited me to her house to celebrate when one of her children received the church sacraments. I thought about this idea and decided to go for it. The soldiers had left, ordering us to stay immobile. But I knew they would come back shortly. The moment was now. The house was only fifty feet away. I rose and headed to the bamboo fence separating our properties. I quickly climbed the fence and fell over the other side. I felt my strength returning; now I was ready to fight for my life.

I knocked on Therese's back door and she quickly opened it. "Thank God these soldiers did not harm you," she said, genuinely concerned. Apparently, she had been watching us.

"I do not know for how long, though," I replied. "They said they will be back. Is there anyone you can call for help? You are my only hope for the moment," I said, literally begging her.

She thought about it and then said, "The captain who lives at the end of the street is a good friend of my husband. I'm sure he can help." I had met the captain on a few occasions in the neighborhood; he was young and seemed to be a good person. But at that moment Therese's phone rang and she picked it up; as she listened, her expression showed concern. I guessed it was her husband. At the same time, I heard footsteps and voices from the street and started to leave. With the receiver glued to her ear, Therese motioned for me to wait. Grabbing a pen and a piece of paper she quickly wrote down the captain's phone number and handed it to me. I wanted to tell Therese I couldn't make a call since my phone line had been cut off by the soldiers. But she was still on the phone and I couldn't wait. I waved her goodbye and quickly ran back to the fence. The steps were getting closer, and I could hear the soldiers talking behind the cypress fence of my property. I climbed over the bamboo fence and then ran back to the house, resuming the exact position in which the soldiers had left me.

A moment later the soldiers had surrounded us. I whispered a quick prayer. It would take a miracle to get us out of this situation alive. I asked God to perform that miracle.

The team leader advanced and began to interrogate us: "Do you know a man called Mbaguta?" I considered his question for a second, wondering how to respond. His grin troubled me, for it suggested he knew something more than he wanted to reveal. I chose to tell the truth. "Yes, I know Mbaguta. I worked with him at the ministry of finance and economy."

Had I known what had happened I would have collapsed in front of the soldiers. At that very moment, I would learn later, Mbaguta's body—along with his wife's—was stacked with thousands of other corpses in one of the numerous mass graves prepared by local authorities. He was a prominent Tutsi, well known in the capital. For many years he had held the position of director general of economic policies, and his name had often been floated on the list of potential cabinet members. But his ethnicity disqualified him. I came to know him at the Institute of Statistics where he taught a class in economics. Despite the age difference, he had become not just a colleague and friend but a real mentor to me, as if we were family.

"Has he ever been at your house?" the team leader continued. I immediately saw where this conversation was headed. My interrogator was obviously looking for any political connection to him. Mbaguta was a member of the Socio-Democratic Party (PSD), one of the largest opposition parties to the regime. Although the government officially recognized the PSD as a legitimate organization, the hard-liners in the regime considered membership an act of treason. I sensed the soldier was fishing for some information that would make me guilty by association with Mbaguta and thereby give him reason to kill us then and there.

"He came here the day of my engagement," I replied. "I made sure to invite my friends and coworkers," I cautiously added. Despite my effort to put forth a confident demeanor, I was shaking.

"Why are you scared?" the soldier asked.

"Because he is a cockroach!" clamored a voice behind us.

The voice, which came from someone new, cracked open the relative quiet like thunder. Then I saw who spoke. His physical stature alone was completely intimidating. Compared to the other soldiers, he looked like a mountain. He wore a military uniform and a chain of munitions around his large chest. Scarier still was the weapon he was holding: a heavy machine gun that looked like a rocket launcher.

The three soldiers spontaneously gave him a military salute, their chests erect. He responded with a more informal salute, and then the soldiers relaxed. Had I been in different circumstances, I would have laughed at this almost comic display of authority.

"Hands up everybody," the Mountain said, pointing his gun at us.

"Who is the head of this household?"

I hesitated, and then replied: "I am."

"Get up and show me the files."

"What files?" I replied.

In response, the Mountain pointed his gun in my back and pushed me into the house. I lost all hope, convinced now that my life was about to end. As I walked into the house, I began to imagine the pain of getting shot in the back, my spine cut into pieces. I had given up defending myself; I just stood there, waiting for the shot to be fired.

But the shot never came. The soldier did not fire. Instead, he said:

"Do you have some money?" For a moment I was confused, not knowing how to react. Was this a trick? "It's not for me. It's for them," he quickly added, pointing in the direction where the other soldiers were standing.

"Yes, I have some money," I quickly replied. I gave him the thirteen thousand Rwandan francs I had. The Mountain took the cash, went outside, and talked to the soldiers. A minute later he came back inside. As he entered the house, his expression was more relaxed, his voice more gentle.

"I'm Sergeant Mukiza," he said. "You are lucky to be alive," he added. "These men were going to kill you." I stood there listening, still frightened by what I had just been through. I couldn't believe the sudden change of events. Was I dreaming?

"I do not know how to thank you," I finally said, in an almost unintelligible voice.

"You should thank Dr. Therese. She called me asking help for you. I'm a good friend of her family, and I respect her a lot. You are really lucky; she called when I was ready to leave. As he walked out of the house, I noted that the three soldiers had already left. "Now, do you have any place to go?" he asked. "I'm certain these men will be back as soon as I leave. And you better not still be around."

I thought quickly and decided to go to the Swiss Village. Thank God, Christine had reminded me of her boss's evacuation offer. By now, I thought, all the expatriates in the neighborhood had taken refuge there. The Swiss Village was conveniently located less than a mile away on the same street as my house. Among the available options, it was the safest place.

But there was something I wanted to do first: if possible, I must try to rescue Christine, assuming she was still alive. When I told the sergeant about my plan, his answer turned my blood cold.

"Are you out of your mind?" Mukiza said. "That is the most dangerous zone right now. The fighting down there is intensifying and there are a lot of casualties already. If you have relatives or friends down there, forget about them. It's over. Besides, there is no way to get there safely. There are three roadblocks in between."

The sergeant's words detonated within me. In the next moment, as if echoing my thoughts, a huge explosion shattered the neighborhood sky. "Get out of here," shouted Sergeant Mukiza, as he ran back down the street. I quickly went back into the house and paused for a moment, wondering what to take with me. I quickly gazed at my new electric stove in the kitchen, then the new couch in the living room. I had bought them in preparation for my wedding. But right now, this equipment meant nothing. What mattered now was staying alive! Still, I thought I should take a few items crucial for the road ahead. Running to my bedroom, I opened the closet and pulled out a small leather briefcase. I quickly checked the contents and found what I was looking for: my college diploma. I thought it was one of the few things that would help me in the future if I made it out of this place. I put the diploma on the bottom of a suitcase, threw some of my clothing and my sister's on the top and ran. On my way out, I grabbed a warm blanket, my new Sony VCR player, and a portable two-plate electric stove. Philippe and Sophanie grabbed a few of their items, and we threw them in the trunk of the Peugeot. Julienne was already in the car.

Not for the first time, the Peugeot refused to start. I put the car in neutral and asked Philippe and Sophanie to push it down toward the street. Meanwhile, I engaged the clutch with my left foot and carefully positioned my right foot on top of both the brake and the accelerator. Once the car started to slope down, I released the clutch and gave a push to the accelerator. The engine coughed, then hummed, then rolled down the driveway. I immediately hit the brakes. Philippe and Sophanie jumped in, and we raced the car as fast as we could. There was a roadblock at the end of the street, in front of the captain's house. I almost turned back but Sergeant Mukiza emerged from the trench on the side of the road and motioned for me to proceed as he removed the wide tree branch blocking the street.

The Peugeot sped off, its passengers praying for the best. We knew the militia was everywhere. We could not rely on Sergeant Mukiza anymore.

The "Swiss Village," where I would find temporary refuge.

11

The Swiss Village

In my distraction I almost missed the entrance to the Swiss Village. After overshooting the Village's gate, I put the car in reverse and backed up. A guard in a blue uniform took my car's plate number and our names before allowing us in. There were several other cars in the small parking lot. Another guard was pacing, keeping an eye on every new guest. He approached and motioned for me to open the window. "Who are you looking for?" he asked in a not-so-friendly tone.

"Jean Marie Sammin," I said, "a Belgian working for the ministry of agriculture. He is expecting us," I added importantly.

The guard spoke into his Motorola radio and received a short answer. "Wait here," he ordered, then disappeared.

I looked around and studied the place. It was beautiful and very clean. I sensed it was safe too. Obviously, the place had not seen any of the chaos that was ravaging the rest of the city. A minute later, two white men emerged from the apartment buildings. I immediately recognized Christine's boss Sammin, a tall and thin middle-aged man. The other man was of medium height and athletically built. He did not bother to introduce himself. I figured he was the manager of the place. He barked some orders into the portable radio he was holding and then turned to me.

"You cannot stay here," he said, without any introductory comments. "The Village is full, and we do not have any space available."

"Then we will just stay in the parking lot," I said. "We have just escaped death; we cannot go back."

"No, you cannot stay in the parking lot; I'm sorry, there is nothing we can do," he insisted.

Sammin approached and suggested that I go to his house down the street. "It's safe there," he said. I wondered whether that was true. Given the choice, I would have preferred staying at the Village. It was very unlikely that the army or the militia would attack a place where expatriates were staying. But evidently we had no choice.

"Get in the car and follow us," the manager ordered.

Before I could say a word, the men were gone. Reluctantly, I followed their VW.

But as we started to leave, a bolt of lightning, followed by a big explosion, hit the whole area with such force that I thought it was an earthquake. Suddenly, a large man in military uniform emerged from across the street and motioned for the cars to stop. I immediately recognized Sergeant Mukiza! He looked agitated. He spoke briefly to the driver of the VW, who immediately reversed the car in the opposite direction. Something was definitely happening. The men in the VW motioned for me to follow them back to the Swiss Village.

"You really want to die, don't you?" Sergeant Mukiza said as I maneuvered to turn back.

I reversed the car and fled back to the Swiss Village. The man driving the VW asked us to stay in the car, and then he took off. A few minutes later he returned, now accompanied by a Rwandan man.

"This is Musa," he said. "He will show you where to stay." With that, he quickly disappeared. I never saw him or Sammin again.

Musa was a small man, with a round, kind face. He looked in his early thirties. He appeared friendly and I decided to trust him. He led us to his apartment, which consisted of a small living room, a kitchen, a bathroom, and two bedrooms. We sat in the kitchen area, where Musa's wife was sitting, holding their infant son. She made us some tea and gave us a snack. Musa told us he worked at the Swiss Village as a housekeeper. He said he lived in Nyamirambo, a neighborhood nearby. Since April 7, however, he and his family had received death threats, and they sought refuge at the Village.

Musa did not think they directly targeted him, but he feared for his wife, who was a Tutsi. He said we should be fine here.

The shelves in the kitchen were furnished with some canned food.

"We have been running low on food in the last week," Musa said. "But the manager promised to buy some more soon." Food was not on my mind. I had no appetite and I was scared. For now, I just needed a safe place to stay.

The apartment's two bedrooms were large and furnished with queen beds. Each room had large windows with a clear view of the street. Musa and his family occupied one bedroom. He gave us the second bedroom. As I put my suitcase into the room, I realized it was now my only possession. But this did not bother me. Though I owned almost nothing, I felt lucky to be alive. I thanked God for the gift of life, which is more precious than any material possession. Thinking about it again from a different perspective, I actually found I still owned everything I really needed: the air I breathed, a heart to love, a brain to think; I still had faith and hope. Yes, I was alive. I wondered, however, for how long. Very soon, I sensed, the expatriates assembled at the Village would leave and only God knew what this place would become.

I had to check on my fiancée. But I also was afraid of what I might learn. There was a phone in the apartment. Hesitantly, I dialed her number; no one answered. After many attempts, I gave up. I felt disappointed but also in some sense relieved. I was not ready for more bad news after all we had gone through already. I went to bed that night totally exhausted.

At five in the morning the following day, there was a knock on the door. It was Musa. He quickly updated me on what was going on. All the European expatriates staying at the Village had departed.

"I can't believe they left us! They lied to me," he complained. "They promised they would not leave us. Now anything can happen; the militia will definitely attack this place."

I too was alarmed. In my naïveté, I had believed the Europeans would not leave us, or at least they would take us to a safer place. Now I understood why Sammin and the village manager did not want to have us in the first place. They certainly did not want to draw the militia's attention—at least before their departure.

"I do not know what to say, Musa," I said. "Let's just hope the Interahamwe do not know that we are hiding here." "That's impossible," he said. "All the night guards here are sympathetic to them. Some actually are Interahamwe themselves. Also, there is a lot of stuff here; they will come to loot and find us."

I knew he was right; but what could we do? There was no place to hide, and it was too dangerous to venture out into the streets.

"Let's just think this through and get a few more people involved. Maybe someone will come up with a good plan."

Although the Village was relatively small, there were a surprising number of apartments on the property. Each of them was housing several refugees. I decided to wake up the other men and see if we could come up with a plan. We met in Musa's kitchen. Fear was visible on everyone's face, but no one had any reassuring ideas. We simply decided to take turns watching the street and eventually alert everybody in case of an attack.

At the Swiss Village, life came to a standstill. More Tutsi people had arrived after the Europeans' departure. I sensed the Interahamwe were watching and would attack us soon. There was no way we could leave. There were roadblocks everywhere, guarded by presidential guards. I started looking for a place to hide in case of an attack. The options were slim.

Outside in the backyard was a small storeroom facing the kitchen door, with five large shelves inside. I thought this was a good hiding place and showed it to Julienne, Philippe, and Sophanie. They agreed and I began to huddle them inside. Sophanie and Julienne were the skinniest, so I placed them on the top shelves. Philippe was the heaviest, and he took the bottom shelf. I closed the door and placed myself on the remaining shelf, above Phillippe's. It was dark and quiet. Even our respiration seemed to have stopped. I could only hear myself think.

In a strange way, I found some small measure of peace in the darkness of the tiny windowless room. I closed my eyes and forced myself to think that I was safe, at least for the moment. The silence around me allowed my mind to withdraw and find peace; it enveloped my spirit in an armor that kept negative thoughts away. I made myself spiritually invisible and therefore strong, invincible.

But as soon as I began to settle down, the painful reality of our situation hit me in the face, and I remembered I was running for my life. I began to pray again. I asked God to shield us from danger, to be with us, and keep the killers away. I prayed that he would offer a sign that he was watching over us.

Someone knocked on the door, and my heart sank, knowing this could be the end. But it was a gentle knock; were the killers trying to trick us? We all stayed quiet inside the storeroom. But after hearing a second knock, I jumped from my shelf, and, with a shaky hand, opened the door.

It was a man nicknamed Murokore, who had been leading prayer sessions at the Swiss Village. His nickname means "the born again."

"What is going on?" I asked.

"You better get out of this storeroom," he replied. "I watched you getting in and thought I should warn you; this is a very bad idea. The Interahamwe are smashing any locked door." He said that earlier in the morning, the Interahamwe searched many houses in the neighborhood and used axes to smash all closed doors."

Without a word, we all descended from the shelves and got out of the small room. At the rear entrance of the main building, I turned and scanned again the whole backyard, searching for a possible place to hide. While doing so, my eyes caught something lying on the ground in front of the house next to the Swiss Village. I drew closer and looked. It was a body. I felt a chill in my spine as I realized that death was so real—and right in front of me! Musa told me later that the body belonged to a Tutsi young woman who was a nanny in that house. When her bosses were evacuated by foreign troops, she was left behind. Then the militia found her hiding in the house, raped her, and executed her outside in the garden.

Murokore followed us to our apartment and invited us to pray. He always kept a Bible in his hands.

"Despite what is happening, I still believe our Lord is good and fair," he said. "Let's respond with faith in him and not fear." He flipped through the Bible, located a passage, and started reading aloud.

Musa and his wife were sitting quietly and listening. Musa was a Muslim, but he seemed to be paying attention to these words. At that moment, we did not belong to different religious affiliations. We were all united, in total humility. We all bowed our heads and listened. When he finished reading, Murokore asked us to hold hands and invited us to pray silently in our hearts. I closed my eyes and prayed for my fiancée, begging God to keep her safe. I prayed for my family, wherever they were, and for all of us at the Swiss Village. I felt good in my heart. The prayers strengthened me; I had never realized how simple words could be so invigorating. After the prayers, we all went to our rooms and waited. There was nothing else to do.

12

A Glimpse of Hell

The night had fallen quickly on the Kiyovu hill. I went to bed but could not sleep. The image of that innocent young woman, whose body I had seen on the Village grounds, kept playing over and over in my mind. Her dreams and her hopes were now gone. I imagined she had plans for the future, perhaps to build a family, have children and even grandchildren. Now all these had vanished. I imagined how she felt when she saw the killers rush on her with machetes and clubs. This image affected me deeply. Soon it might be our turn. There was no doubt the militia would soon attack our place. I got up and went outside. The air was cool but not refreshing. In my pocket I could feel the piece of paper that my neighbor Therese had given me—the phone number of the captain living at the end of our street. I hesitated an instant but then decided to call the captain, wondering if he could offer us one more lifeline. Back in the apartment I dialed his number. No one answered. I returned to bed but remained awake.

The next morning, April 13, I got out of bed before dawn. I tried calling the captain again. No answer. Something told me we were running out of time. My body was rigid, but my mind raced wildly in search of some way out. In the kitchen I poured some coffee, and for an instant felt myself coming back to normal. Back in my bedroom I looked out over the street. I could hear the sound of car engines mixed with human voices and laughter. Life outside the Swiss Village sounded normal, but it was anything but normal.

Suddenly, there was a noise. Then another noise. Voices. Low voices, as if someone was trying not to be heard. Then steps: steady, careful steps. I rose carefully and slightly opened the blinds.

When I was a child, I always feared the sight of red ants, advancing in a line. The picture before me reminded me of that fear. There were many of them, quietly advancing toward the building—not ants, but men. Several dozen of them, maybe fifty or more; I could not really tell. They were advancing quietly and confidently. Their faces showed no emotion. Many of them wore military uniforms, but only a few had boots on their feet. I figured these few were government soldiers. They carried guns and were leading the way. The rest of the group wore sneakers and carried machetes and clubs. They were militiamen. Seeing these men and knowing they were coming to kill us was the most frightening thing I had ever seen.

I rushed outside and told whoever I met. In a few seconds the news spread, and everyone ran for his or her life. I saw people climbing the wall separating the Village from nearby houses and disappearing on the other side. My cousin Philippe tried but could not make it; he was too heavy. I gave him a boost and he disappeared with a loud thump on the other side of the wall. Murokore came running and easily climbed over. He paused at the top of the wall and offered me a hand. But I did not take it. I realized that Julienne was missing. I ran back to the apartment, ignoring Murokore's pleas to join him. The heavy steps were getting closer. People were screaming all around. It was total confusion. I spotted Julienne in a corner; she was like a sheep lost in the woods. Suddenly we heard shots, mixed with screams. For a second, Julienne and I stood there, immobile, not knowing what to do. I looked around. There was nothing to protect us. Without thinking, I pulled Julienne and we ran toward the back of the apartment.

There was a low window in front of the kitchen. I set a foot on the window's ledge, and climbed to the top of the roof, which was low and flat. Julienne hesitated. I told her to bring a chair from the kitchen and use it. As she climbed, I grabbed her hand and pulled. Her hand was sweaty and slippery, so I leaned down further and grabbed her by the waist of her jeans. A few seconds later, she too was on the roof—just in time. In less than half a minute, the killers descended upon the place in force. For an instant it felt like an earthquake.

A man was barking orders, telling his men to look everywhere. Then he said something that surprised me: "Find him, I know he did not get far. His car is here." Actually, there was only one car in the parking lot: mine. I was the main target; I was the prey they were hunting. But who was this man hunting me down? His voice sounded familiar. It must have been someone who knew I was hiding at the Village. He sounded furious. I listened carefully to see if I could put a face or a name with his words. He spoke again and I listened. His voice was hard and sharp as a machete. But who was he? Suddenly, it hit me! It was unmistakably the voice of the captain living on my street, the man that my neighbor Therese tried to call three days earlier to come to my rescue—the same man I had tried to call as well. For an instant, I felt my spirit leave me. Fear invaded every part of my bones. For the first time ever, someone in particular wanted me dead. It felt as if something were severing a precious tie with humanity. My mind took in a new and sad truth: that evil need not come in the form of a hostile stranger; it can take the form of an acquaintance. From my position on the roof, I did my best to stay immobile and quiet.

The fiber cement roofing was attached to its frame with long nails, which made it difficult to get comfortable. Julienne began tossing around, and I feared her noise would expose us. After a moment, we got used to the roof and settled down. Beneath us chaos reigned. Mad men erupted from nowhere, shouting and destroying everything in their path. They caught a man called Joseph, whom they began interrogating.

"Where do you live?" one militiaman asked him.

"Nyamirambo," Joseph responded

"And why exactly are you here?"

Joseph hesitated, not sure how to respond to this obvious question. I found myself trying to formulate an answer if asked the same. To lie was dangerous, but to tell the truth was bound to be fatal.

"What brought you here?" insisted the militiaman.

"I heard the rebels had approached the capital, and I feared they would capture and kill me." It was a lie. All the men around laughed out loud. At that very moment, I knew he was finished.

"I will tell you why you are here," said the man. "You are a cockroach!"

Joseph began to say something, but they ordered him to shut up.

"I'm sending you a cockroach," the man shouted to a group outdoors. I imagined they were militiamen carrying machetes and clubs. "You know what you have to do."

As soon as he heard this, Joseph ran. The killers ran after him, shouting.

"Shoot the bastard!" one man yelled. Then I heard a shot.

"Shoot him again, he is still moving!" another ordered. I heard another shot, then silence.

The sound of trucks brought me back to reality. Many trucks, which made a deafening noise, started heading toward our place. Down in the apartments, someone began giving orders: "Pack the heavy items first." They were looting. It was a relief to know that a lust for material goods was offering some distraction for the killers. I did my part to keep still, carefully avoiding the nails on the roof, desperately hoping that the dust would not provoke my allergies and bring on a sneeze that could betray me.

The looting continued throughout the afternoon. The longer the better, I thought. But every minute seemed like an eternity.

Was I destined to come to a violent end? It hardly seemed possible; I was not ready to leave this world. I thought of Christine, of our dreams, and of our future together. I forced myself to believe that I would survive for her, and this became my focus from that point onward. I didn't have a plan; I knew I was scared. But from that moment, I was determined to think with my heart and use every single cell of my brain to fight for my life and for my love.

13

Is This Really Happening?

At last darkness fell on the capital. The trucks left the Swiss Village, and the commotion in the apartments below was replaced by a deafening silence. I was back to my loneliness. As odd as this may sound, the afternoon noise had enveloped me, shielding me, and to a large extent distracting me from my fears. Now I was exposed, alone, and vulnerable. A single noise could trigger the end. I sensed that the killers remained in the area. Perhaps some of them hid in dark corners, waiting for a sound or for their prey to emerge.

I still could not believe what I had seen and heard. How could people become such savage beasts and how could the rest of the world do nothing about it? We were living in the twentieth century, not the Stone Age. Rwanda was a not primitive territory but a recognized country—and a Christian nation! What happened to the civilization I once knew? I thought of the expatriates who were evacuated from the Swiss Village earlier. Where were they now? Where was Sammin, Christine's boss? Were they speaking on our behalf, trying to gather support for us from their powerful governments, or had they already forgotten about us?

I had no plan, but I still had a choice. I chose that I would not become a victim and fortified my will to survive. I said to myself, "You survived the presidential guards, you will survive the militia as well. Do not let despair overcome you!" Hiding on the top of the roof was not an enviable position, but at least I was still in one solid piece. Many were already dead, and some were captive and awaiting their fate. I forced myself to think that I was lucky, that I was going to make it. I would realize my dream of creating a family and having the children I had always wanted.

As quickly as these resolutions emerged, they were overtaken by negative thoughts. A dark voice within kept telling me that I was a fool to have any hope, that I would not escape: "You are in big trouble! Soon it will be over; you will be history."

For a minute I considered running from this place. With the cover of the night, I might find ways to get out of the city, and head to the South, to my hometown. But I knew this was not a feasible plan; I could not leave my fiancée and my sister behind. Finally, I gave up thinking, and turned instead to prayer. One more time, I pleaded for God's protection, for me and my loved ones. I asked God to be our shield, to keep the killers away. I felt so helpless, so powerless, and trapped. I humbly put myself into his hands and prayed for strength, for hope, and for a way out of my desperate situation. I had never prayed so deeply.

At around 1:00 a.m., I heard voices again. The gate opened and a vehicle entered the property. By the sound of the engine, I could tell it was a pickup truck. They started loading whatever they had come for. Twenty minutes later, the vehicle left the property, no doubt with some valuable assets. The cold became intolerable. I touched Julienne's arm to comfort her. She was so cold I feared she would get sick. I had a warm blanket down in the apartment. But how could I get there without compromising our safety? A part of me thought it a foolish idea. Nevertheless, I decided to go get the blanket. But what if the looters decided to come back for more stuff? More anxieties invaded my mind. I waited another half hour and decided to get down.

My steps on the concrete floor were like steps on the moon: heavy and slow. I knew I did not have time to waste. Stiff from lying on the roof, my whole body was functioning in slow motion. If caught, I knew I could not run. Cautiously I walked to the kitchen door. Despite the darkness, I could see the chaos in front of me. The floor was covered with glass debris, papers, canned food. . . . The kitchen cabinets were destroyed. The electric stove and the refrigerator were missing, as well as the kitchen table and the chairs. The chaotic mess revealed the fury of the killers. Walking

On a return to Rwanda in 2013, demonstrating how I climbed on top of the roof at the Swiss Village to escape the militia.

against the wall to keep my balance and to avoid shards of glass scattered in the middle of the kitchen, I crossed the corridor and entered my room. The bed and the mattress were gone. The closet was smashed down. The floor was a disaster. Surprisingly, my luggage was still there, its contents untouched. Apparently, the looters did not want used clothing. And then I saw the blanket. But the sound of an approaching car made me jump. I started looking for a place to hide. Not finding any, I hated myself for taking such a big risk. But after a minute, the sound slowly faded away. I quickly grabbed the blanket and went back to my hiding place. Climbing up to the roof seemed more difficult this time. Julienne was asleep but her body was freezing. I covered her and myself. The warmth of the blanket brought me back to life. The sky was completely dark. That darkness was my best ally—one of the few friends I had.

Meanwhile, Julienne slept peacefully, her thin body squeezed between the iron screws. Her breathing was irregular but quiet. I had to be ready to intervene in case she started snoring. I could not stop thinking about what awaited us, and what to do. I kept going through the names of people I thought could help me. I thought of men from my native region of Nyanza and with whom I had worked in the past couple of years in a newly created association to promote the economic interests of the region. They were moderate Hutu and possibly had Tutsi connections within their families. One of them was Paul Rusesabagina. Just recently we had held a meeting at the Diplomates Hotel, where Paul was the manager. The hotel was located less than a mile from the Swiss Village, but with all the roadblocks, there was no way I could reach it, even assuming Paul was there.

The night passed slowly, as I tried to recall happier memories: growing up with my family in Nyanza, my boarding school at the French Lycée (just down the hill from the Swiss Village), studying at the Institute of Statistics. I thought about my family. Were things as bad outside of the capital? As medical professionals my parents had helped so many people and touched their lives. Often on weekends people would knock on our door to say thank you. In the past thirty-five years, my parents had worked in almost every hospital in the country. They had received medals for their loyal service and dedication to the well-being of Rwandan citizens. After retiring from his work in the hospital, my father had opened a small pharmacy in our hometown. As for my mother, she was often praised for providing exceptional care to pregnant women and for successfully delivering babies even in the most complicated cases. Many grateful women would bring their infants to our house to show my mother how healthy they had grown. "Febronie has the touch of an angel," people would say about my mother. She was an angel indeed, and I loved her more than I could ever show. Surely my parents would be all right.

In the midst of memories of friends and family my thoughts continuously returned to Christine. I closed my eyes and brought to mind her gentle smile, warming my heart. I thought of the day she caught my eye, of the first steps of our romantic journey, of the way our love grew day by day. And then I remembered the last words we had exchanged on the phone, the fear in her voice, and then the scream and the gunshot that followed. Was she alive and safe? I could not bear to imagine the alternative.

Eventually the morning light rose on the hills of Kigali and the sky began to lighten. Never before had I feared the dawn. Now, once again, it meant exposure. Soon the city would awake and the hunt would resume. I turned again to prayer. But I knew prayer alone was not going to be enough.

14

Gamble with Death

Julienne saw them first; three men in green military uniforms, standing on the side of the street up the hill, just above the Swiss Village.

"They saw us!" she cried. She started to sit up, but I quickly pushed her back down.

"What are you doing?" I said. "Let's keep our position; maybe they didn't see us." But I didn't believe my own words. There was no way they could have missed us.

The man in the middle had binoculars. He was watching something on the opposite hill. The other two carried long guns on their shoulders and stood still as if waiting for orders. Suddenly, the man lowered the binoculars and started to descend the hill toward the Swiss Village. The other men followed, adjusting their guns on their shoulders. They would get to us in a matter of minutes.

I felt the end approaching fast. There was no escape. Julienne and I joined hands and began to pray. I was overcome by a surge of emotions. I could not stand the thought of seeing my younger sister tortured and killed.

Finally, I heard heavy footsteps and people talking. I could not hear what they were saying. Long minutes passed. Nothing happened. The men no doubt knew our hiding place on the roof. My entire body remained on high alert, like a twitching squirrel sensing danger in the woods. Five, then ten, then twenty minutes passed. Still nothing. Maybe God had answered our prayers; maybe the time of our death had not yet arrived.

Suddenly, a crazy idea hit me. When I explained it to Julienne, she looked at me in disbelief. "Are you out of your mind?" she said. She was probably right; no doubt my plan was suicidally reckless. But time was running out. We had to act. My plan was this: simply to go straight to the soldiers, head held high, as if I had nothing to hide. And then? Luck or grace would provide.

Climbing down from the roof, I walked confidently over to the security guard at the Swiss Village, who looked at me as if I were a ghost. He was holding a small portable FM radio and listening to the extremist radio RTLM.

"What do you want?" he asked without lowering the volume of the radio. He sounded defiant. His breath smelled of tobacco and alcohol, and his eyes were bloody red. I could read his mind: he was looking at an enemy. His expression loosened, though, as I pulled a twenty-dollar bill from my pocket and handed it to him. (I still had all my US dollars in my pocket.)

"I want you to find the three men in uniform and tell them I need to talk to them about something important," I said. He grabbed the money and grumbled something unintelligible. After he had disappeared around the corner, I ran back to the other side of the building and helped Julienne descend from the roof. Her hands were ice cold.

"They will kill us right on the spot," she said, understandably scared.

"Don't worry," I said, as convincingly as I could. In truth, I was wondering if this crazy gamble would turn out to be the biggest mistake of my life. But I knew staying indefinitely on the roof meant certain death. We had to take a risk to have any chance of survival. .

In a few minutes the guard returned, followed by three angry-looking men. Judging by their uniforms and haircuts, two of them were government soldiers; the third, wearing sneakers, no doubt belonged to the militia.

"Why did you call us?" the militiaman asked, taking the lead over his colleagues. Before I got the chance to respond, he continued with another series of questions: "By the way, who are you, and why exactly are you here?"

I told him my name, hoping it would not ring any bells. It did not. Though I was hiding, I could not admit it. So instead I chose to answer the first question only.

"I called you because I need your help." I hesitated, choosing my words carefully. I had to be clear and not sound like I was hiding anything.

"I live just one kilometer from here in a government house," I said, emphasizing the word *government* with a forced air of self-importance. "But I had to leave this morning because I was told the area could be the target of enemy fire at any time."

"Who told you that?" interrupted one of the soldiers.

"The bodyguard of the captain living on my street," I lied without any hesitation. "I'm sure the captain would have helped me, but he was not home. They told me to come here because it's safer, but I'm not sure it is. So I have a proposal that will benefit everybody."

Only silence followed. This could be a good or bad sign, depending on what I had to say next. The men looked at me suspiciously, as I continued to talk.

"I need to get out of here as soon as possible. But I cannot venture alone in the streets. I need a military escort. This is a difficult time as you know, a time of war. If you help me, I will pay for the service."

"How much do you have?" asked one of the soldiers. I liked the question. The plan was off to a good start.

I pulled a hundred-dollar bill from my pocket and handed it to him. The man took the money but did not look as excited as I had anticipated. My hopes dimmed. "Tell us the truth. What are you doing here?"

Again, I repeated the story of why and how I left my home, afraid of the enemy's fire. While the soldiers interrogated me, the militiaman watched me suspiciously from a distance. With a sudden movement, he turned and left. I could tell he had a volatile temper. I watched as he talked to the security guards down the street. A few other men sitting on the side of the street got up and joined the group. They talked in low voices. Their whispering was not a good sign. All these men carried machetes. No one had a gun.

Though I began to sweat, I tried to keep my body from trembling.

The discussions down the street were becoming more animated, and the men with the machetes were growing restless. Some of them were visibly drunk. I forced myself to think of different options, but my mind was empty. Suddenly, I remembered what Sergeant Mukiza had told me a few days ago. "Money is your best companion right now." There was no time to waste. One of the soldiers seemed more understanding, or at least less defiant. I pulled another hundred-dollar bill from my pocket and put it in his hands.

"Please, help me. I'm sure you will not regret it."

Then the other soldier, who had been quiet so far, spoke.

"What do you want us to do with these bills? This is not real money we can use!"

It took me five long seconds to understand what he meant. To him, US dollars had no value. As surprising as this may sound, only local currency was real money. This had not occurred to me. I had to think quickly about how to respond.

"This is not a problem. I have a friend at the Diplomat Hotel. You escort me there, and he will give you the money." I had no idea how the Diplomat Hotel came quickly to my mind. But as I thought about it, it was not a bad idea. Maybe Paul was there and he could lend me some money.

"How much?"

This was no time to bargain, and I was determined not to lose an inch of the ground I had just gained.

"A hundred thousand Rwandan francs," I said, without think-ing. It was a large sum, but the number did not matter; anything just to get out of the Swiss Village.

Before they could answer, the militiaman came back, charging at me like a fuming bull.

"Cockroach, come here!" he commanded.

I tensed as I watched him approaching.

Fortunately, before he could get to me, the two soldiers inter-vened and took him aside. They stood there talking and then argu-ing among themselves. After a few minutes, they came back. I held my breath and waited for the verdict.

"Let's go," they said. Two simple words, full of meaning, full of life; two words from heaven. "Do you have a car?" the soldiers asked.

"Yes I do," I said enthusiastically. The younger soldier went in the apartment building and came back with a bottle of whisky. He took a gulp, passed the bottle to his colleague, who passed it to me. I have never been a liquor drinker, but at that moment I gladly accepted. Refusing to share a drink could be seen as an insult, and I did not want to upset the men holding our lives in their hands. I took a sip and passed the bottle back to the soldiers. The liquid descended in my chest and restored my strength. I watched in disbelief as the men emptied the bottle as if it were water.

"Let's go," I suggested. I knew it was quite dangerous to hang out with drunken men carrying guns. For a moment I found myself standing next to the militiaman while the two soldiers stayed behind. His face and bloodshot eyes projected a frightening picture. I was afraid he was going to change his mind, and I felt a need to coax him along. Removing my two-plate electric stove from my car I offered it to him. He took it, looked at it with indifference, and then tossed it to the side of the small parking lot.

The two soldiers climbed into my car. They asked the militiaman to take the front passenger seat, while they sat in the back with Julienne in between. I picked up my electric stove, put it back in the car, and started the engine. Thankfully, the old Peugeot started up without complaint, and a minute later we were on the road. The soldiers pointed their guns through the open windows as a demonstration of force.

Although Kayuku Street next to the Swiss Village was usually busy, now it was empty. The grass on the side of the road seemed taller. I felt relieved as we sped away, leaving behind the place where my sister and I had nearly met our death. But deep down I lacked confidence. So far my "plan" was working out wonderfully; but I was making it up as I went along, and I could not be certain how far this would take us. A dog crossed the street just before the intersection of Kayuku Street and Paul VI Avenue. As I slammed on the brakes, the soldiers on the back seat swore angrily, and made as if to shoot the dog. As I turned right on Paul VI Avenue, a nauseating odor hit my nostrils, and we all quickly closed the windows. There were probably dead bodies in the bushes along the road.

The area was as quiet as a cemetery. This was one of the oldest and most prestigious avenues of the city. Along Paul VI were most of the Western embassies and other beautiful villas built during the colonial era. I had always found peace walking along this road on a weekend, but now the place was deserted. The surrounding houses looked empty and miserable. We passed a military Jeep full of angry-looking, armed soldiers. They were obviously heading for Nyamirambo, a zone at the edge of the city known for its relatively large Tutsi population. I looked in the mirror and caught a glimpse of terror in Julienne's eyes. We had relatives in Nyamirambo.

We passed the Vatican mission on our right. Deserted though it was, the sight of the mission nevertheless gave me some hope, some connection to a civilized world. Maybe somewhere, someone was watching and would make the case for our rescue. A few more seconds on the road, however, and my hopes vanished. Just as I had feared, about half a mile down Paul VI Avenue, a roadblock appeared. It was guarded by what looked to be a half-dozen soldiers. A large iron bar was set up across the road. It was reinforced with long nails that would shred even the most solid tire. As we approached, a soldier advanced, put up his hand, and ordered us to pull over. A Jeep with a mounted machine gun was parked on the side.

"Show your IDs, everyone!" The words were hard and sharp. My ID was the last document I wanted to share with anyone, as it showed my ethnicity. At the Swiss Village, the soldiers and the militiaman had not asked for identification. Maybe they assumed I was not a Tutsi, judging by my physical appearance and my brash self-assertion. But the time for hide and seek was over. Things looked very serious. Without showing any hesitation, I removed my ID and handed it to the soldier. I feared the soldier would hear my heart beating. But then, amazingly, he did not open it to look. After glancing at the cover page, he read aloud the name of my home province, Butare, and then returned it to me without comment. *"N'abasilikare, muzane ibyangombwa!"* ("soldiers, show your IDs as well!") Here things got complicated. While the two soldiers in the back seat removed and presented their IDs, the militiaman refused to cooperate.

"I do not have an ID," he finally said, visibly irritated.

"What do you mean you do not have an ID?" retorted the military officer.

"I just told you I do not have one!" the militiaman arrogantly shot back. Not amused and very angry, the officer said, "What do you have then to identify yourself? What makes us believe you are not a cockroach?" "I was just given a regimental number," the militiaman responded.

"I do not care about regimental numbers," interrupted the officer. "Get out of the car. Now!"

As the militiaman refused to cooperate, the officer pulled his pistol. Three more officers joined in. Finally, the militiaman got out of the car, and they ordered him to sit on the ground.

"Chauffeur, wowe komeza" ("driver, you can go"). As I sped away on Paul VI Avenue, I looked back in the mirror and saw the officers beating the militiaman.

"That idiot is playing with fire," one of the soldiers with us said, referring to the militiaman. "This place is close to the central military command. That's why this roadblock is guarded by sergeants, not privates," he added.

As we passed the building of the military school on our left, we saw sandbags stacked along the fence. A few men carrying guns positioned themselves randomly throughout the property, and many hid inside the trenches. I refocused on the street and looked straight ahead, knowing that a prolonged look of curiosity could lead to trouble.

I took the next left heading toward the plateau, where many government dignitaries lived. I avoided the Boulevard de l'Armée, which passed in front of the military school and led to the infamous "Camp Kigali," where government soldiers had killed ten Belgian "blue helmet" soldiers just a few days earlier. Instead, I continued straight and then turned left onto the Boulevard de la Révolution. I could not believe we encountered no other roadblocks. A minute later, I entered the parking lot of the Diplomat Hotel. A military truck was leaving the parking lot and I hesitated. Once it disappeared from our sight, I got out of the car but instructed my sister to stay inside. The soldiers got out as well and wandered in the parking lot, while I walked into the hotel's lobby.

The Diplomat Hotel was a beautiful multiple-story building that sat on the flat plateau on top of the Kiyovu hill. The destination of high-end tourists and senior business executives, the hotel usually had fewer people and less noise than its counterpart, the Hotel des Mille Collines, which was within walking distance from the commercial district. That day, however, the Diplomat had a flurry of activity and felt chaotic at every turn. The lobby looked like the platform of a train station at the peak hour. Men, women, children, soldiers, and civilians intermingled with loads of luggage everywhere. Most looked exhausted, having spent several days there. Some men talked loudly in small groups, while women and children sat on their luggage or on the few available chairs. Men in military uniforms, preoccupied with the events around them, came in and out of the hotel. I stepped into the lobby, trying to avoid eye contact, hoping no one would recognize me.

Walking straight to the reception desk I asked for Paul, the manager of the hotel. My plan was to see the manager and convince him to lend me a hundred thousand francs. In case he needed a guarantee, I thought my car would suffice for collateral.

For a second the foolishness of this plan struck me. I had met Paul only on a few occasions; he was only an acquaintance, not a close friend. Why would he lend me a hundred thousand francs, assuming he had the money somewhere in the hotel's safe? But there was no time to analyze this further.

"Paul is no longer here," the receptionist said. "He moved a few days ago to the Mille Collines Hotel."

Now what? What would I tell the soldiers? That I could not deliver on my promise? They were not completely sober, and they could shoot me and Julienne right there in the parking lot.

Before I could decide what to do next, a voice addressed me: "Did you have to flee your home, too?"

Looking around, I saw a middle-aged woman. She spoke with a northern accent, and I immediately recognized her: Gaudence Nyirasafari, director of the National Population Office, which oversaw all issues regarding family planning. She was one of the few high-ranking women in the country. She taught a class on demographic statistics that I took in college, and her agency had once hired me and two other classmates for a summer job.

Her question took me by surprise. I gave a vague response. "My family does not have a home anymore," she said in a desperate tone. "The rebels have bombed our neighborhood in Rugunga, and we cannot even go to our hometown in the North, because the region is now under their control. We really do not know where to go."

I could not believe she was confiding in me! She sounded really shaken. Other people in the room showed the same anxiety. I had come to the hotel thinking only of my desperation, but now I witnessed the despair of high-ranking government officials who suddenly found themselves homeless. At that moment I realized that the current government had lost control of everything. Since everybody seemed worried about their own survival, I felt less worried that they would notice me as I struggled to work out my own.

Although safer than in the Swiss Village, I still felt vulnerable in the Diplomat Hotel, and I kept reminding myself that I needed to get out as soon as possible. Gaudence was still talking to me, but I was deep in thought, trying to figure a way out. I was about to excuse myself when a soldier in a green uniform approached.

"Major, when are we going to get out of here?" asked Gaudence.

"I will be evacuating a group of nuns to Gitarama very shortly," the major responded. "But my colleagues will continue to evacuate people in the afternoon."

This meant that in a couple of hours all the people would leave this hotel, exposing me once again unless I left with them. But how could Julienne and I pass all roadblocks with our Tutsi IDs? How could I go without my fiancée? I had to find a way to get out of this place—quickly. The major left and I hurried after him, realizing that he offered me some new leverage. After all, he had seen me in good company and could think I was one of them.

"Major, I need your help," I said, as I caught up with him. He seemed nervous and hurried.

"Like what?" he asked, without slowing down.

"Can I join your convoy?"

"We are full," he said

"I have a car, if you do not mind. . . ."

"Then just follow us," he said, impatiently interrupting me, and not even asking where I was going. With that, he headed to the door. I literally ran after him. This was a one-time opportunity if I wanted to get out of this place. I wondered what to tell the two soldiers, but I could not think of anything plausible. I ran to my car as the major's Jeep and a minibus exited the driveway. Julienne was still in the car, dozing on the back seat. The soldiers were not around, and without wasting a second, I started the engine and drove off. As I left the main gate of the hotel, I saw the two soldiers sitting on the edge of the street, drinking beer from a bottle. When they saw me, they ran after the car, ordering me to stop. Too late. I already had a significant lead. As I accelerated behind the Jeep along the Boulevard de la Révolution, I watched in the mirror as they faded in the distance. I could only imagine their rage.

As we drove ahead, the Kiyovu plateau was now incredibly quiet. My car and the convoy ahead were the only vehicles on the road. The major pulled over and entered a house along the boulevard. I pulled over behind him and waited. I did not like the wait. Finally, he returned and the convoy proceeded on its way. The Jeep took the next right and entered the Boulevard de l'Armée.

We passed the Hôtel du 5 Juillet, a flat villa that sat in a large wooded property. The villa functioned as a residence of the first president of the country in the 1960s and early '70s. Although called a hotel, the public never had access to it. Under the Second Republic, the government used it for cabinet meetings and receptions.

Now it looked deserted and miserable. A minute later we passed the St. Michel Cathedral, where I worshipped every Sunday. The Cathedral appeared unscathed, which did not surprise me considering that the Bishop of Kigali had close connections to the regime.

A minute later the convoy stopped at another roadblock. Again, a chill went down my spine. A soldier approached the major's Jeep and they spoke. The roadblock opened, and the minibus and the Jeep passed. Just when I approached the roadblock, they started to close the gate. But then the major stopped, opened the Jeep's window and spoke to the soldiers. Obviously, he had power. They immediately opened the gate, allowing me to pass. While the Jeep accelerated down onto the Boulevard de la République, I slowed down to let him go. If there was a chance for me and my sister to live, I had to separate from the convoy and pursue an alternative option. The major certainly did not care. I waited for his Jeep to disappear behind the French Cultural Center and then onto the Boulevard de Nyabugogo toward the south; I turned left to enter my new hiding place: the Mille Collines Hotel.*

It was April 14, 1994.

Hôtel des Mille Collines

---

* The Mille Collines Hotel was depicted in the 2005 Hollywood film *Hotel Rwanda*.

15

The Mille Collines Hotel

Contrary to my expectations, the parking lot of the hotel was almost empty. This probably meant that most of the foreign expatriates usually at the hotel had already left. Nevertheless, the hotel lobby was still busy. Journalists, done with their reporting duties, were packing away their cameras and eagerly preparing to leave. While several UN soldiers surveyed the surroundings, a few Rwandan civilians, with terror in their eyes, talked to the journalists about the horror they had witnessed.

"I'm looking for Paul Rusesabagina" I told the receptionist.

He ignored my question and went on the other side of the desk to chat with someone. I chose not to be offended, for my mind had bigger preoccupations. I saw another receptionist whose face looked familiar. He made a call and after a moment, told me where to go.

Paul stayed in a suite in one of the large wings of the hotel. He greeted me and my sister at the door and invited us into his living room. His wife, Tatiana, emerged from a room and greeted us with a hug. I knew her from my hometown because she had worked with my parents at the Nyanza hospital as a nurse. I was happy to be with familiar faces. We sat in the living room, talked about the situation in the city, and watched world news on the TV. I did not talk about the money I had promised the soldiers I had left at the Diplomat Hotel; I had no intention of seeing them again. I just wanted a room. A few other people came and we shared news about the situation as it was being described by the foreign media.

Everybody quieted down when the French TV channel began to broadcast news about the worsening situation in Rwanda. I felt like a passenger on a ship caught in the middle of a violent storm at sea, helplessly witnessing smaller boats sinking around us. The reporter quickly switched to other world news. I had expected the channel to give a lengthy account of what was happening and sound the alarm for the world to be indignant and eventually intervene. It seemed our situation was just one item on the TV station agenda. But for us it was reality. After the news, we started leaving the room in silence. Paul called reception and asked them to find me a room.

On my way out I met Louis, an old acquaintance, who worked for a local bank. A moderate Hutu, whose life was at risk, Louis was terribly depressed by what he had seen on his way to the hotel: a band of ferocious young militiamen cruelly executing scores of young Tutsis, possibly high school or college students. Louis cried as he described the horrific ways they were hacked to death.

The hotel receptionist assigned my sister and me to room number 208. It was a comfortable room equipped with a queen bed, a desk, a TV, a phone, and a very clean bathroom. But the beautiful accommodations were the last thing on my mind. Having a chance to finally catch my breath, I began to feel again. Every ounce of my body was now focused on my fiancée. The last time I had heard from her they had just been attacked. Was she safe? Or still alive? I had no idea. I approached the phone, hesitated, and then made the call. The phone rang a hundred times but nobody picked up. I decided to try later.

My growling stomach reminded me that I had eaten nothing in the last thirty-six hours. Hoping the restaurant was still open, I headed upstairs. I had no Rwandan francs, but I still had a few hundred US dollars and hoped the Mille Collines would take foreign currency.

I had frequented the hotel's restaurant before and loved it. But it looked different now: cold, dark, and almost empty. I asked an employee if they were open. He looked at me from head to toe, grumbled something, and then disappeared. Another employee saw me and came over. He graciously told me they were not running a normal restaurant schedule but had some leftovers in the kitchen. I was amazed to find a polite person in this wild world, knowing the brutal inhumanity going on outside the hotel. The leftovers consisted of some rice and red beans. I grabbed a plate for me and Julienne and headed back to my room.

I tried again to call Christine, but nobody answered. For several minutes, I sat there, paralyzed and lost in thought, wondering what to do next. Emotionally, physically, mentally, and spiritually worn out, I laid my head on the pillow and decided to rest. Within a moment I was fast asleep.

I saw the men advancing quietly but quickly. Every one of them carried a machete. Their leader trailed behind, a pistol in hand, pushing a handcuffed prisoner. Although they covered the prisoner's head with a hood, I could see it was a woman. Suddenly the group stopped. Their leader advanced and shot in the air, and then shouted, "Listen up, cockroach. I know you are out there. Get out or we will kill her."

In a brusque movement, he uncovered the prisoner, and when I saw her face, I jumped forward, screaming like a warrior on the offensive. It was my fiancée, and I refused to let them harm her. With all my energy, I went toward the leader and kicked hard with my foot, but apparently, I missed, for I did not feel any contact.

Opening my eyes, I found that I had fallen off the bed in my hotel room. My sister hovered over me with a frightened look on her face, wondering if I had lost my mind. For a moment I didn't know if I had just had a bad dream or awakened to one.

Night came quickly, covering the Kiyovu hill in total darkness. Unlike most of the surrounding buildings, the Mille Collines had not lost electric power, but most of the occupants kept the room lights off for fear of drawing attention. Leaving my room and wandering through the hall, I saw fear and anxiety on all the faces I encountered. In the dim lights their bodies projected long, ghostly shadows on the walls, creating a haunting presence. I took the stairs and went on the top floor, where I had a view of some parts of the street above the hotel's parking lot. I saw figures in the dark moving around, some with flashlights. These were members of the Interahamwe militiamen, surrounding the hotel. God help us, I whispered.

Voices were coming from the ballroom. As I approached I saw a group of men and women praying. A man was holding a Bible in his hands and talking to them. He spoke with eloquence and conviction. Although their faces expressed the pain of their tormented hearts, the group seemed to have hope and gratitude in their eyes. I joined them. The pastor was praying for the occupants of the hotel, asking God to keep the killers away. His words somewhat comforted me and calmed my nerves.*

Very early the next morning, I got up and wandered the hallways. Through the windows overlooking the street I could see that the Interahamwe were still there. Their numbers seemed to have increased. I bumped into some old acquaintances who had lived their own moments of terror before arriving at the hotel. We told our stories and exchanged the latest news on the radio.

"Things are not looking good," one of the men said. "The army and the militia will storm this place at any time. The rebels are gaining ground, the Rwandan army is losing, and they may take revenge on us."

The thought of an imminent attack on the hotel kept playing in my mind throughout the day. I knew the hotel was safe for now simply because of the UN flag that floated on its roof. But it was only a matter of time before the killers learned that only a handful of UN soldiers were staying at the hotel. Only God knew what would happen to us then. Eventually some people got scared and went back to their neighborhoods. An old friend of mine was among them. Days later we heard he was killed.

---

* For our entire time at the Mille Collines, the number of people praying on the top floor increased every day. They were from all religious denominations, but they always came together, prayed, and comforted one another, like one family.

People continued to arrive. They were mostly women and children, hungry and exhausted after several days of hiding. Their stories confirmed the gravity of the situation and the barbarity of the assailants. One of the women said she survived killings in the Gikondo sector. This is a neighborhood I had lived in for many years after graduating from college, so I paid attention to what she was saying. The woman added that unfortunately many other people who fled to the local Catholic church run by Polish priests did not survive. Immediately upon news of the president's death, soldiers and militiamen had started killing Tutsis and moderate Hutus all over Gikondo. Hundreds of Tutsis fled to the church, hoping to find sanctuary. But soldiers went in the church, checked identity cards to identify the Tutsis, and brought in hundreds of Interahamwe militia who started killing everyone inside with machetes and clubs. For several hours, screams could be heard all over the area. Men, women, and children were hacked to death inside the church; a few who managed to escape were finished off outside in the yard.

I listened as the woman described that scene of unimaginable horror. Was this the Rwanda I grew up in? What had happened to humanity? What happened to the Christian values this country had been taught for a whole century? I thought of all these innocent victims, of the fear they experienced and the pain they endured in their final moments. I thought of the parents who tried in vain to shield their children from that horrible death, of these children decapitated under the pews. I then thought of good friends of mine, Jean Baptiste Kayitana and his wife, Francine, who lived in Gikondo with their newborn baby. Were they in the church? Had they escaped the killings?

Other people came from Rugenge. This was Christine's neighborhood.

"The city counselor there is crazy," a woman was saying. "She ordered the militia to search all houses, capture all the Tutsis, and execute them."

The news made my fears grow. If Christine was still alive, the militiamen would surely find her. I decided to call. Again, there was no answer.

But an hour later, when I dialed the number, someone picked up the phone after the fourth or fifth ring. I could hear the angry voice of the landlord resonating through the line.

"I told you not to call. You can put all of us in danger!" he yelled. But I did not take offense at his tone, for he added something I desperately needed to hear.

"We are all fine; but you need to understand that we need to stay quiet here," he said, still screaming at me. I screamed as well, but for different reasons. I was happy now. I would have given the man a big hug if I were there. I thanked him a thousand times, as if he had raised Christine from the dead.

But the news was not reassuring; militiamen surrounded them on every side, watching every movement in the neighborhood. I had to do something, but what? Different plans flew through my head. My brain had never worked as hard.

In one scenario I would drive down to Christine's place around three in the morning and leave the car several yards from the house. I would then walk to her window and urge her to get out as quietly as possible. We would then walk back to the car and drive to the hotel. As I looked at all the angles and details of that plan, I did not like it. Something was off. How could I assume the militiamen would be slumbering? With thousands of militiamen out there, they were undoubtedly taking turns patrolling the streets and guarding the roadblocks. I shook that plan from my mind; I needed another one.

16

Love Is Stronger than Death

There were a few gendarmes staying at the hotel, guarding a well-known Hutu army officer, Major Cyiza, a human-rights activist who was staying at the hotel for his own safety. Since he hardly left his room, his armed guards could occasionally go out and bring to the hotel people trapped in low-risk neighborhoods. They did not, however, rescue people for the sake of compassion; they did it for money. I doubted they would take my case because Christine's neighborhood had become very dangerous. But I had no other option; I decided to ask them.

The guards stayed on the first floor; I found the room and knocked on their door. The gendarme who answered the door was courteous, even friendly, which surprised me. I quickly explained what I wanted.

"I can't promise anything," he said. "I will need to talk with my other colleagues."

"Wait," I said, as he was about to close the door. "You help me and you won't regret it." I said these words with an air of self-assurance, as if I held the key for his future well-being.

He hesitated for a second, about to say something, but then shut the door.

At around 11:00 a.m. on April 18, the phone in my room rang, and I picked up. The landlord was on the other end of the line in a complete panic.

"We are leaving. If you can come get her, do it right now," he said, shouting.

I struggled with what to say next, but he insisted, "You need to come get her. We are leaving soon."

"What's happening?" I finally asked.

"Things look very bad here. My family and I are leaving shortly, and we can't bring Christine with us." Still shouting, he repeated those words: "We can't take her with us!"

"I will come get her as soon as I can," I said.

"You need to come right now," he said again. Then the line went dead.

I left my room running. Some people on the second floor ran after me, thinking we were under attack. I stopped and explained.

"What? You are going outside?" one of them shouted. "Are you crazy?" another said. I did not have time to argue. And I could not change my mind anyway. I headed downstairs onto the first floor. People I crossed stared at me as if I had gone insane. I knocked on the gendarmes' door and waited. No answer. I knocked again, harder. Nothing. Two, three, four minutes passed; I knocked a third time. This time, the door opened and a tough-looking man appeared in the doorway.

"What do you want?" he asked, visibly annoyed. He was wearing military pants but no shirt.

"Please, I need your help," I begged. "I spoke with your colleague the other day about helping me bring someone here."

"We are not doing this anymore," he said, showing an even more sour face. "It's too dangerous!" And then he shut the door.

I stayed a few minutes, wondering what to do next, hoping the gendarme would change his mind.

After a while, I decided to leave. I could hear people talking on the second floor. I did not want to see anybody right now. I knew what they would tell me. They would try to advise me against going outside. Some would do it for fear of being exposed to danger. I would not blame them. Armed militiamen surrounded the hotel. I heard people had already been killed on their way to or from the hotel. But I did not want to hear any of these arguments. I chose to go upstairs to the top floor to a corner that looked out on the beautiful panorama of the city. But I was not focusing on the beauty of the place. I was reflecting on the challenges that lay ahead, and the possibility of dying while rescuing the person I loved the most. Love for Christine meant more to me than my own life. I was not afraid. Closing my eyes I offered the most spontaneous, most sincere prayer I had ever given.

My mind was racing in every direction. I did not see any way forward other than begging the gendarmes for help. I had to get them involved. I was not sure how, but I was determined not to take "no" for an answer. I ran back downstairs to the gendarmes' room and knocked with insistence.

When the door opened, the gendarme I had spoken with the other day appeared. He looked more relaxed than his colleague.

"I need your help," I said, "and I will pay for the service," I added in a hurried tone, fearing a negative response.

"What do you need again?" he asked, as if we had never met.

"I need to bring a friend of mine here." He thought for a moment and asked, "A male or a female?" I hesitated a second, wondering what difference this would make. Maybe gender determined the price to charge.

"A female," I answered. He frowned, as if deliberating if he could take my case or not. I held my breath.

"Where exactly is she?" I told him the place in Rugenge, close to the old *payage*—"the tollbooth."

"It's not far from the hotel," I quickly added.

"How are we supposed to know the house?" he shot back.

"I will come with you," I said firmly.

"You realize it's dangerous," he warned.

"Yes," I said. He studied me for a moment but said nothing. He probably thought I was a fool.

"Wait here," he finally said. "I need to consult with my colleagues." He went inside and a minute later he came back with his two colleagues. The tough-looking man, whom I met earlier, was still bare chested.

He did not waste time to name his price; it was more than I had anticipated but I accepted, relieved. This was no time to bargain.

While the gendarmes got ready, I went to my room and called the landlord's house. He picked up at the first ring.

"She is ready," he said. "Please hurry!" he added, now surprisingly calm.

"I will be there shortly," I assured him. "Do you have any food left in the house?"

He paused, probably wondering why someone staying at a hotel would need food from his house. But the hotel's supply was almost gone. "There is a bag of rice, why?"

"Can she take it with her, if you do not mind? We will need it."

Two minutes later, my car exited the gate of the hotel, with three soldiers pointing their guns through the open windows. Some people from the hotel looked at me through the windows of their rooms. I could read their minds: "Poor guy; he lost his mind." I did not care what others were thinking. I was deaf; I was blind; I was driven by a powerful feeling, ready to confront any obstacle that stood in my way. That feeling was uncontrollable, unstoppable, even in the face of death.

Down the road, I hesitated on what route to take. We had two options, and neither one of them seemed safe. Turning left onto the Boulevard de la République, though shorter, certainly had more risks. The Boulevard led to the Rond-Point, the central roundabout that connected the capital to different regions of the country. No doubt government soldiers and militiamen guarded the area and fortified it with roadblocks. Something told me we should continue straight ahead, down onto the Avenue du Roi Baudouin. *(I would learn later that, had I taken the left turn, I would not have even reached the roundabout because there was a large presence of armed militiamen in the area.)*

The road straight ahead was practically deserted and very quiet; I held my breath as I passed the building of the National Bank on my right. To my surprise, it was not as heavily guarded as I had imagined; maybe the money and the gold deposited in the vaults were already gone. My armed passengers waved to the few soldiers wandering in the large garden. All looked good so far.

As I raced down the avenue, I saw no other cars on the road. This was not good, as my car could easily be spotted. The neighborhood was as quiet as a cemetery. The silence of the Kiyovu hill was perturbed only by the echo of my car's engine and by sporadic gunshots heard from the hills surrounding the capital. I took a deep breath to relax the tightness of my chest. I felt exhausted. I forced myself not to think and focused on the road. My arms felt like rigid sticks as I tightly gripped the steering wheel. The soldiers in the car were quiet, emotionless. I wondered if they would do anything to protect me. Probably not.

The loud sound of thunder startled me, and I ducked, hitting the brakes at the same time. It was only a storm and I continued down onto Kayuku Street. It started raining hard as I crossed the Boulevard de l'OUA and entered the dirt road leading to the landlord's house. At the same time, I saw people running, seeking shelter wherever they could. Most were carrying machetes. They were militiamen.

I needed to act fast. The sense of urgency injected a rush of adrenaline in my veins. The road was getting flooded and slippery, but I decided not to slow down. Suddenly I bumped into something so hard that the soldier on the front seat almost bumped his head on the dashboard.

"Be careful," he shouted, not happy at all.

I apologized while putting the car in reverse in order to maneuver around the obstacle. We had hit a huge tree laid across the street, which served as a roadblock. Fortunately I saw a narrow passage left on the side and steered around it. Then I saw a dead body on the side of the street. I decided not to look at it and focused on the street. More bodies came in my view as I advanced. A horrible scene, almost impossible to avoid: people with clenched hands, their faces still expressing shock and agony.

A minute later the landlord's house came into view, appeasing my own agony. As I entered the property, I saw Christine, running toward us, holding a small bag containing her belongings, and a kilogram of rice in a plastic bag. Her face revealed fear and anguish. Behind her I saw someone else, but I did not expect him. It was Maurice, the brother of Christine's friend and roommate Laetitia. I had no objection taking him with us, but for the soldiers it became a problem.

"You did not tell us there were two people," complained one of the soldiers.

I ignored the comment. I couldn't afford to start an argument. As soon as the door closed, I took off. The soldiers did not pursue the matter. Just when I passed the roadblock, some of the militiamen who had gone to take cover down the street because of the rain came running. But I was far ahead. I watched in the rear-view mirror as they ran behind the car, brandishing their machetes. I feared the engine would stop running, since the Peugeot 305 model had a reputation for misfiring under acceleration. On many occasions in past years the car stopped on me in the middle of the road without any warning, and I worried it would betray me now at this critical moment. But this time it kept flying, as if sensing the danger behind us. I was so grateful for its loyalty.

None of the passengers in the car dared to say a word. Christine had joined her two hands in a praying position, her frail body squeezed between Maurice and one of the soldiers. Maurice was immobile, like a statue, his big eyes fixed on the road ahead. We all knew anything could happen anytime. I chose not to think. I just kept going, rigid like a robot, emotionless like the soldiers. The moment felt like the climax in a suspense thriller. Never in my life had I imagined a situation like this. And I certainly did not know where and how I found the nerve to stay calm and sane in those conditions. I was frozen on the outside, but inside I was super active, burning with the determination to get away from death. My body was driven by a powerful, inside force that was at work in me. Never on my own could I have attempted such a daring rescue.

When I reached the asphalt road, I knew we had the advantage. The militiamen chasing us were at least a hundred yards behind us. They made a lot of noise to draw attention to us. But occupants of the few vehicles going down the street ahead seemed to have problems of their own. I crossed the Boulevard de l'OUA and entered Rue Député Kamuzinzi. Government soldiers guarded the gate of a residence, which was on our right, and at the approach of my car, one of the soldiers moved closer to the edge of the street and waited. I panicked. The gendarme in the passenger seat waved and the soldier retreated. He must have assumed we had a dignitary on board. A minute later I turned right onto the Avenue du Roi Baudouin and flew to safety toward the Mille Collines Hotel.

We left the parking lot running, our heads kept low as if exiting a helicopter; we hurried inside the building without talking. Once in our room, Christine gave me a long embrace full of meaning; it was a humble celebration of love's victory over death. I held her firmly against my chest, a protective grip around her frail body. At that very moment we became one flesh. My heart still pounding in my chest, the images of the last half hour would not leave me. It was like a dream. Julienne looked at us, astonished. I could tell she had given up on me. I couldn't believe this was real. Everything could have gone wrong. Yet even as we grieved the death that surrounded us, we made it safely back to the hotel without grave incident. Some may call it pure luck, but I knew something had just happened; something powerful, meaningful, although I could not understand it. I have always wondered what a miracle looks like. I had just experienced one.

17

Praying the Novena

Christine was still shaken and terribly cold. She had lost half of her weight. "You are very skinny," I told her. A weak smile materialized on her face, but she did not respond. Instead, she pulled me toward the bathroom, closed the door, and knelt down on the floor. Without hesitation, I did the same. She started praying and I joined in. The prayer lifted me up. It was spontaneous, sincere, right from the bottom of my heart. I had never expressed devotion to God the way I did at that moment. It was a special moment of communion and closeness, during which I made genuine promises to renew my faith and trust in him.

"I'm going to start a novena," Christine told me, as she concluded her prayer.

Although I prided myself on being a good Catholic, I had never heard that word. "What's that?" I asked. She explained that a novena is a series of prayers that are said for nine days to ask for God's favors. She added she would be saying the prayers for as long as we were stuck at the hotel. I welcomed the idea. Right now we needed prayers more than anything else.

Christine and Maurice were still shaken; but gradually they collected themselves and started telling us their story. Maurice had kept a diary in which he recorded details of their journey. He was visiting from his hometown of Kayonza in the East and was stuck at his sister's house. He and Christine told us they learned of the president's death on the morning of April 7 through the national radio. The landlord came and warned them immediately, asking them to stay quiet. They did not need any warning. They knew that the army and the militia had already started killing Tutsi people in their neighborhood and that they too were in danger. They heard that an elderly woman living next door had been burned alive in her house. They knew that their own physical features—their thin faces, long noses, and skinny necks could betray them. They knew any killer would recognize them as Tutsis.

Maurice's brother-in-law was a Hutu, and he was not supposed to feel scared. But he was still terrified, and so was the landlord, who was a Hutu as well. The murderers could find both men guilty and assassinate them for hiding Tutsi "cockroaches." Neighbors kept watch on everyone's activities, and killers patrolled everywhere. So the landlord urged everyone to stay inside and told his neighbors that his annex was not occupied. He told his tenants to keep quiet at all times and to stay away from windows and from common areas such as the living room. In order to avoid raising suspicion, they could only shower or flush the toilet when it rained.

As I listened to their story, I understood why the landlord had expressed anger whenever I called Christine; he had to walk to the annex through the backyard to call her, and Christine would have to walk the same distance to answer the call, all the time at the risk of being seen by government soldiers who patrolled the area or by militiamen.

I asked Christine what happened on April 10, the very last time we spoke on the phone. As she described the incident that occurred that day, I realized I almost got her killed. She said that when I called, she went to the landlord's house to answer the call; as soon as we started talking, she heard someone saying soldiers were approaching the house; then several gunshots were fired just outside. Christine screamed and started looking for a place to hide. The landlord's wife panicked, pushing Christine outside and locking the door; a woman working for the landlord's family screamed, warning Christine about their aggressive dog, which was not on a leash. The dog barked fiercely and threatened not only to betray them all but to wound Christine. The aid begged the woman to let Christine back in the house.

"I do not care if the dog bites her," the woman screamed back.

Christine started running, and just when she had reached the annex, she heard a gunshot, and the dog stopped barking. She heard soldiers questioning the aid, asking her to produce her ID card.

Then they told her, "Had you been a Tutsi, you would be lying next to this dead dog."

After such a grueling ordeal I would have loved to take Christine to the restaurant, but following the expatriates' departure, the hotel had stopped cooking for guests. Now the guests, all of whom were local residents fleeing violence in their neighborhoods, took turns in the kitchen on the top floor preparing the evening meal. Stoves were priceless commodities, and people spent hours and hours in the kitchen waiting for their turn to cook.

Fortunately I still had the electric stove that I had packed before leaving home, saving us the hassle of waiting in line in the kitchen. We cooked the rice Christine brought, and with some peanuts someone had generously provided, we made a sauce.

For several days rice and peanut sauce were our only meal. Eventually we learned that a few people at the hotel could go out and occasionally get some vegetables and even meat at the market in downtown Kigali. These were Hutu who had fled their neighborhoods, either because they had Tutsi wives or could be targeted themselves as moderates. One of them was an acquaintance of mine who had been my neighbor several years ago around the time I started my career in Kigali. He promised to get us some food, and we gave him money. Unfortunately when he returned to the hotel, he only brought us a few kilograms of salt. He explained he couldn't find anything else. We swapped the salt for more rice and peanuts from other people at the hotel. It was evident we would soon run out of food. Meanwhile, the hotel was getting more crowded.

There were new faces every day. We had no idea how many people took refuge at the hotel, but judging by those who attended prayer sessions in the evening or Mass on Sunday, one could estimate the number to be at least a thousand. I started seeing people I knew: high ranking government officials, diplomats, businessmen, employees in the public and private sector, and many others. As the number grew, RTLM, the radio that fueled hatred to

When water to the hotel was cut off, we relied on the swimming pool.

the extremist segment of the population and the militia, multiplied its attacks against us, asking the Interahamwe to keep an eye on the hotel, which, RTLM reported, was hiding "cockroaches." We expected an attack at any time.

The other threat the hotel faced was food shortage. Unless we could find ways to get more supplies, people were going to die of starvation. The Interahamwe surrounding the hotel were certainly waiting for that moment, when we would be forced to get out of the building in search of food. In face of this imminent threat, a brave man named Victor Munyarugerero found ways to bring corn and beans into the hotel. He was a man of faith who always kept the hotel and its occupants in his prayers. He was viewed among us as a hero.

With more food entering the hotel, the kitchen on the top floor became a point of rendezvous and exchange. Christine and Julienne were often there, and they made numerous friends. There they met a mother of three small children, Daphrose, who always waited patiently before having access to a stove to start cooking for her family, which caused her three young children to cry incessantly. While people were patient and courteous for the most part, there were a few who unscrupulously always cut in line. Those who were too well mannered like Daphrose to fight for a stove could wait a whole night. Thankfully, we still had the two-plate stove, and Christine was always sharing it with others.

There was not much one could do at the hotel, yet we were all always exhausted. Men spent their time talking in the hallways, exchanging information and speculating on what might happen next; women and children often stayed in the overcrowded rooms, away from depressing news. Often, in the hallway, I bumped into other people I knew directly or by reputation. The hotel was home to individuals of different backgrounds and social standing. But we all shared the same threat, the same fears, and the same hopes.

I avoided telling Christine what I heard in the hotel corridors; the news was often frightening. Nor did I talk about the future. Instead, we talked about the past. I knew much about her and her family, but I was always eager to know more, or to go over the same stories again and again. Like many from her native Bugesera region in the southeast of Rwanda, the story of her life was one of struggle, but also of triumph over adversity. So I listened intently as she recalled her life in Bugesera.

Christine grew up in a family of nine children. Her father, Straton Mutabaruka, was a teacher in a local elementary school. Teaching jobs were almost the only opportunities the local Tutsi population had access to. Teachers' wages, however, were very low, and Christine's large family lived very simply and hardly made ends meet.

Christine's mother, Nathalie, supplemented the family income by working the fields every day while also attending to other domestic chores. "She is an angel," Christine said of her mother, her voice softening. "She did not get far into school, but she is the best adviser I have ever had; I learned a lot from her; often people in the community come to her for advice."

She also knew the value of education. Mother Nathalie wanted all her children to go to school, which was far from their home. She would wake them up very early in the morning to get ready for the long walk. As Christine recalled, the rocky path was tough on their bare feet, but they often had to run for fear of being late. The headmaster was a severe man who always waited with a long stick in hand to punish tardy students.

Christine worked hard in school and earned good grades; but when the moment came for high school, she was not admitted. This was not a surprise, as the political system did not give Tutsi children the educational opportunities they deserved. When school started in the fall, her only option was to retake the last year of primary school in the hope of better luck the following year.

Meanwhile, however, her family learned of the opening of a new high school in Kigali, funded by a generous Tutsi entrepreneur. After passing the entrance test, Christine was admitted. Her father sacrificed everything and took loans to support her. For the next six years, she attended the school, while staying with her uncle Laurent Kayijamahe and his family in Kigali. Those years were filled with fond memories.

Upon graduation from high school, Christine took a job for two years as an administrative assistant at a public high school in the northern city of Gisenyi before thinking of college. Unfortunately, life changed when the war started in 1990. As it had been in the past, the Bugesera region was labeled as the bastion of "cockroaches" and targeted by government forces. The tranquil atmosphere disappeared very quickly. Violence against Tutsi erupted from nowhere. Christine's generation was now experiencing the same atrocities their parents had faced in the 1960s. She had just started attending college in Gisenyi, but that northern region of Rwanda was not any safer for Tutsi people. It was the native region of President Habyarimana and other dignitaries of the regime who were averse to the Tutsi. She recalled a moment that gave her the scare of her life. One day when returning to school, she got a ride from a French woman, Joelle Magnier, who was the director of the public high school with whom she had worked in Gisenyi a couple of years back; another Belgian woman rode with them. Before reaching the city their car was pulled over by a group of soldiers at a roadblock. One of the soldiers carefully checked ID cards; while the two Belgian women's documents were returned, Christine's ID was not. Instead, the soldier put it in his pocket and asked Christine to step out of the vehicle and ordered the car to proceed. But Joelle refused to leave Christine alone with the soldiers. The soldier was caught off guard and was perplexed by Joelle's defiance. Reluctantly, he returned Christine's ID, but not before spitting in her face. She still felt goose bumps when she recalled that close call.

It was in 1993 that Christine and I started planning for our future together. But Christine was determined first to help her family stay safe and well. She found a job at a Swiss-sponsored development project in Kigali, rented a two-bedroom house in Rugenge, a modest section in the center of the city, and enrolled four of her younger siblings in school in Kigali. By that time her younger sister Clementine had just finished high school and had started teaching in elementary school in Bugesera. Her graduation was timely, since Christine would need her to stay with the younger siblings once she started her own family. Soon Clementine got a job in Kigali and moved into a hostel rented by Catholic nuns within the compound of the Lycée Notre Dame de Cîteaux, a high school for girls located on the central plateau of Kigali. All of Christine's plans were falling into place.

The younger siblings were thrilled to live in a safe place in the capital, away from their troubled Bugesera region. But their happiness was short lived. They had to return home when the capital was plunged into chaos in February of 1994.

Now Christine was particularly worried about her sister Clementine, who was last seen at the Lycée. Was it safer there than at the Mille Collines Hotel? We didn't know. But what if we did nothing and something happened to her?

Once again I turned to the gendarmes on the first floor, and this time the negotiations were easier. No one needed to accompany the gendarmes, since they knew where the Lycée Notre Dame was located. We agreed on a price, and, before we knew it, Clementine was brought to the hotel. She came with another young woman from Bugesera who had been visiting her when the terror started. Our hotel room was now full, at triple capacity. We did not mind.

18

Searching for the Way Out

Everyone at the Mille Collines Hotel tried to find a way out of the country. Whoever had a friend or a family member abroad tried to reach them. They wanted to make some noise and let the world know about the situation. But we did not have an organized plan for our evacuation. One evening I decided to go fishing for information.

In the corridor, I bumped into a UN soldier and spent a few minutes chatting with him. "If you can find a letter of recommendation from someone abroad," he said, "maybe we can do something." It struck me that the UN was sticking to administrative formalities as in times of peace. How were refugees at the hotel supposed to get the paperwork? My thoughts immediately went to my friend Theopiste Butare in Switzerland. Looking for a phone with an international line, I learned there was one downstairs in the fax room.

At the first ring Theopiste picked up the phone. Without any delay I quickly explained the reason for my call and gave him my fax number and a list of all the people in my room. He promised to send me a letter of recommendation. In the afternoon the fax arrived. I immediately took the letter to the UN soldiers' room. When I knocked on the door, no one answered, but I slid the paper under the door, and later in the evening I returned to check if they received the document.

"Yes, we received it," said the blue helmeted soldier as he popped his head through the partly open door.

That evening, we attended a Mass in what used to be the ballroom, on the top floor. Many people came, whether they were

Catholic or not. We were all in desperate need of hope. Only prayer could provide. Monsignor Nicodeme, a Tutsi priest hiding at the hotel, usually presided at the liturgy. The room was quite full, the atmosphere warm, and the spirits elevated, in contrast to the tense situation in the capital. Another Catholic priest and a pastor from a different Christian congregation also prayed with us, and they also shared their reflections after the readings. Sitting there among that crowd made me feel good. The Mass was our source of strength and hope. As I sat there, I realized that our desperate circumstances made us humble and led us to pray in a deep and sincere way. I had always asked myself why we need to pray to God. Does God not know our needs before we even ask? Now I knew the answer: we need God more than he needs us.

At the end of the Mass there was an announcement: a wedding ceremony would take place the following week.

"I encourage those young men and women among us who are engaged to consider receiving the sacrament of marriage," the priest said.

At the end of the Mass, as Christine and I left the room that was now our place of worship, a woman approached us and said, "I heard you are engaged. Why not consider getting married next week as well?"

Christine and I exchanged a look. We knew what the woman was thinking. Like many people at the hotel, she had lost hope in any chance of survival. She was wondering, "Why not get married if so little time is left?" But I never surrendered to helplessness. If we woke up early every morning and lined up at the swimming pool to fill our buckets, wasn't it a sign that we desperately wished to live? Later at night, we thought of the woman's proposal and reached a conclusion. I did not want to get married in a state of desperation. Christine felt the same way. We had hope, and we forced ourselves to think we would live.

Since that moment, we started hiding from that woman. She was for us the symbol of desperation. Whenever we saw her around, we would avoid eye contact and get away. A week later, the entire community gathered to celebrate the planned wedding ceremony. Two couples got married, and a baby was baptized.

In the morning I heard some noise outside our room and decided to go check it out. People started running down the stairs, and the first person I crossed in the corridor told me what was happening. The UN mission had some news to share with us down in the lobby. I immediately informed everyone in my room, and we all headed downstairs.

When I got there I saw a UN soldier standing on a chair, surrounded by hundreds of refugees—men, women, and children. Nobody wanted to miss the announcement. The soldier then started reading names from a piece of paper. As we had missed the introduction, I asked the woman next to us what was going on.

"They are reading names of the lucky people who will be evacuated," she said. "The UN has reached an agreement with the Rwandan military to use the airport to evacuate refugees in possession of letters of recommendation from abroad." This was great news since we had produced a letter of recommendation as well. But I wondered why we were not informed of the event.

As the soldier read the names, the lucky ones jumped for joy and started hugging one another. Soon they would leave this dangerous land and enjoy freedom and safety abroad. The UN soldier slowly read the names, often repeating them because of his unfamiliarity with long Rwandan names. The names were in no order, so I expected my name to be called anytime. I could not hide my excitement. I gently squeezed Christine's hand and waited with expectation.

Half a dozen government soldiers stood at the entrance of the hotel, and I wondered what they were doing there. What I saw next scared me the most. An officer of the Rwandan army standing next to the soldiers started taking notes on a legal pad. Why was the officer writing down the names? Why could he not simply get the list from the UN mission? Immediately my intuition kicked in. Something was wrong.

Within a short time, the reading of the list ended; they simply never called our names. The UN officer then started to explain the next steps, putting the list in his pocket. I stood there stunned, deeply disappointed; I was somewhat angry at the UN mission for not including my family in the evacuation plan. But at the same time I was anxious and suspicious about this operation.

Soon the lucky chosen ones descended from their rooms with their belongings and boarded UN trucks waiting outside. Visibly happy to get out of the hotel, they left without looking behind, avoiding all eye contact. Ten minutes later, the convoy left the hotel, led by a UN tank waving a white flag. Almost instantly, RTLM, the extremist radio, began broadcasting the news and reading the names of those leaving. Everyone at the hotel knew what was about to happen.

"God help them," someone whispered.

It did not take long to know the fate of our friends. The UN convoy came back to the hotel with the passengers tearful, shaken, and—in many cases—wounded. They all left the trucks and went quietly to their rooms, their heads down, their faces still expressing shock and fear. Later, we sat with some of them and listened to their story.

They had barely gone one mile from the hotel when the convoy stopped at a roadblock. Several militiamen, armed with guns and grenades, ordered the UN soldiers to surrender. When the blue helmets resisted, the militiamen shot the vehicles' tires, climbed in the trucks, and requested ID cards of everyone inside. As the UN soldiers tried to take control of the situation, a period of chaos followed, and the militiamen beat and wounded several people in the trucks. Miraculously, government soldiers intervened and negotiated with the militia, allowing the convoy to return to the hotel.

After that grave incident, the morale of everyone at the hotel plummeted. We now knew the UN could not protect us. With our resources almost exhausted and our energy gone, we knew our final days were drawing nearer. Most turned to their spiritual lives. Prayer groups started to meet, and Masses were offered more frequently. Many attended these events, united not only by a common faith but also by fear.

Rumors started circulating that the military wanted us to leave the hotel and go back home. We knew this meant death. When we did not comply, they cut off the electric power and the water supply. Some said that this decision came from Colonel Bagosora, chief of staff in the ministry of defense, reputed to be a hard-liner within the regime. Although in time the electric power returned, we had another problem: the water supply was dwindling. Thankfully the hotel had a swimming pool, and we started using pool water for cooking, washing, and flushing the toilets. In time, we developed a plan to use the pool in the most efficient way possible. We began taking turns, one family at a time, getting our daily bucket of water. Within a few days, however, the water level was reaching the bottom of the pool. Knowing we had to do something quickly, the hotel personnel secured a truck to bring more water to the pool. Days later, the army confiscated the truck. But Mother Nature brought us a solution: rain. Residents at the hotel saw the rain as God's response to the army. "Moses struck the rock and water came out of it, and the people of God drank," someone said at the evening prayer.

The month of May came with troubling news. As the rebels of the Rwandan Patriotic Front captured major strategic points in and around the capital, the security of the hotel began deteriorating gravely, making everyone tense. Rumors of an imminent attack on the hotel began to circulate. When wandering in the corridor of the hotel one afternoon, I bumped into an acquaintance who had explosive news: the RPF had just captured the Kanombe airport and the nearby military camp, forcing the army to retreat.

Although this meant a defeat for the government soldiers, it also meant more trouble for us. In order for the soldiers to get out of the city, they had to pass through the center, where our hotel was located. Because they knew we were hiding in the hotel, we feared they would take revenge on us. The next twenty-four hours could be the most dangerous yet.

Despite my fears, I did not want to alarm Christine. As I climbed the stairs, considering the worst-case scenario, I tried to think about a place for us to hide. Suddenly I heard a huge explosion, as if the hotel was blowing up. Everybody plunged to the floor. We heard screams and saw people running. Everybody started stampeding toward the basement. I rushed into my room, but everyone had left; Christine and Julienne had followed the crowd. I ran downstairs as well. People streamed from everywhere like a violent torrent. A UN soldier hurried past me, jumping four or five stairs at a time. His blue helmet fell, but he kept running. When I reached the basement, it was already full. I searched for Christine and Julienne but couldn't see them anywhere. I saw many of my friends, visibly traumatized, as if they had seen the devil itself. More people kept coming, and we waited, in silence, for about twenty minutes. Then someone shouted: "You can come out now!"

Slowly we emerged from our hiding nest. Christine and Julienne came from nowhere. Everybody was shaken, and nobody went back to their rooms. Instead, we regrouped in the hotel's corridors, listening to one another's theories about what happened. It appeared that a rocket had hit the concrete wall of the hotel, on the side facing the swimming pool. Had it hit the windows, many people would have been killed. Nobody knew where the rocket came from, but many saw this as a warning sign from the military; and we all waited for an attack to come.

Over the next several days, anxiety at the hotel was at its highest level. To make matters worse, our food and water supplies continued to deteriorate. Militiamen still surrounded the entire area. We knew it was a matter of time before something grave happened. Only a miracle could change our situation.

Toward the end of May we started seeing UN officials, government officers, and other men in suits coming and going from the hotel, alerting us to something happening. I needed to know what was going on. No matter how confidential talks between UN representatives and the armies in conflict were, someone at the hotel always knew something. I approached a group of men talking in low voices.

"There are negotiations in progress to allow an exchange of refugees between the government and the rebels," someone told the group, saying the information came from a UN soldier staying at the hotel.

"If things go well, Mille Collines residents will be sent to a region now controlled by the RPF; believe me, the government has a vested interest in the exchange since many of their family members are trapped in areas controlled by the RPF."

Although deep down I had no faith in the UN's ability to organize anything of this magnitude, I still felt a surge of hope. As I reflected more on this information, I started to believe it. I suspected already that the genocidal government had kept us alive for strategic reasons; the Mille Collines Hotel was the focus of Western media attention and was too visible. The government needed to obscure the fact that a genocide was under way. Attacking the hotel was certainly not in its best interest. Now I knew of another incentive to keep us alive. There were captives to exchange on both sides! When I told Christine about this possibility, a jolt of hope illuminated her face for the first time in a long time.

On May 25, the UN mission organized a general meeting, which was attended by all the hotel residents, UN blue helmets, and some other officials I did not recognize. People packed into the room on the top floor of the hotel and waited anxiously to hear the news. The announcement confirmed the news I had heard. The UN had put in place an evacuation plan to take us to a nearby town already in the hands of the Rwandese Patriotic Front. Evacuations would begin the next morning. No mention was made of negotiations or exchange of refugees, but we were asked to provide the UN mission with our names as quickly as possible. Afterward, and not surprisingly, many felt suspicious. In light of the recent debacle, there was not much faith in the UN's capacity to evacuate us safely. Still, I had reason to believe that this time might be different. For one thing, it seemed plausible that the Rwandan government had a vested interest in the exchange.

I did not waste any time. I wrote all our names on a piece of paper and slid it under the door of the UN officers' room. I went to see Paul to let him know we hoped to be leaving and to inquire about the hotel's payment terms. I had not yet paid any of the bills charged to my room, and given the circumstances, I wondered if I should. Paul indicated that he would not require an immediate payment; any guarantee I could provide would suffice. I gave him my car registration.

19

The Swap

The next morning, May 26, was evacuation day. But something happened and it was postponed until the following day. Once again, the residents panicked and rumors started circulating. On May 27, we woke up before dawn, ready to go and hoping this time that nothing would stop us.

Forty days had passed since Christine arrived at the hotel and forty days since she had started her novena prayers. Early in the morning, people started descending to the reception area, their few belongings in hand. I stood in a corner, watching carefully for any sign of trouble. I did not see any.

A couple of trucks were parked in front of the hotel, each guarded by two armed blue helmets. In the lobby, a UN officer advanced and, after requesting our attention, began reading names. My name was called first, then Christine's, and the rest of the occupants of our room. I was not surprised they called us first, as I had immediately contacted the UN mission after our general meeting. We immediately headed outside. I jumped in the first truck, then helped Christine and the rest of our group climb aboard. Thirty more people piled in. As soon as all trucks were full, the doors closed and the vehicles started moving. Most refugees started praying. Some held rosaries in their hands. A Rwandan army vehicle followed behind us.

We quickly left the hotel behind us, passed the French Cultural Center, and entered the main road leading to the airport. Surprisingly, all roadblocks had been removed. Moments later we reached the well-known Sopecya roadblock, where the first evacuation from our hotel had failed weeks earlier. No roadblock was there either. Apparently, the militiamen took seriously whatever agreement had been negotiated. With the road ahead still uncertain, we turned left toward the Kimihurura hill. As we approached another infamous roadblock, at a place called Kimicanga, I risked looking through the truck tent and saw a few militiamen on the side of the road, still brandishing their machetes menacingly, but now allowing us to pass; the roadblock had been pushed aside. There was still one more dangerous place. As we reached the top of the Kimihurura hill, the headquarters of the presidential guard, we all held our breath. We saw no other vehicles on the road, except the UN convoy.

A minute later, we saw another UN truck coming from the opposite direction. Packed to at least twice its capacity, this lonely truck moved slowly, painfully. Filled with men, women, and children, all mingled with bags, mattresses, and other household items, the truck seemed to have been loaded in a hurry. The occupants looked scared and exhausted. Most likely they were Hutu civilians from the other side of the war zone controlled by the Rwandan Patriotic Front. Now I knew that the "swap" was indeed taking place. We had just entered the no-man's zone between the belligerent armies. The Rwandan army vehicle that had followed us stopped there.

A mile away we saw the parliament building, an unbelievable sight that showed how brutal the fighting had been. The walls were seriously damaged by mortar rounds and bullet holes. But I was filled with incredible hope. The massive building marked an important frontier. As we passed it, an RPF army vehicle started escorting our convoy. One of the UN officers said, "We just entered the RPF-controlled area. Your ordeal is over, my friends."

He must have been surprised when no one in the truck showed any kind of excitement. Many of our fellow refugees at the hotel were still behind and certainly in danger. Also, we felt too exhausted to feel much of anything. He made no other comment, leaving everyone to his or her thoughts. As for myself, I did let out a long sigh of relief. Maybe our miseries were truly over.

The convoy passed through the eastern part of the city and silently proceeded into rural Kigali. The countryside was beautiful, but I was stunned by the emptiness and quiet of the place. There was not a soul to be seen. The grass alongside the road had grown taller, and the surrounding banana and coffee plantations had become bushes. Everyone had left the area. We were all alone.

By mid-morning the convoy entered the eastern town of Kabuga and came upon a large property. The UN officers then asked us to get out of the trucks. We saw a large house of solid stone built on the top of a hill. This was our destination. The house had several rooms, but there was not a single piece of furniture in the entire house, which made it feel larger. Each room could contain ten people sleeping on the floor. As soon as we finished settling in, we heard footsteps outside, then saw several serious-looking young men in uniform taking position around the house, armed with guns.

The soldiers were skinny and tall, and their darkened skin indicated long exposure to the tropical sun. It did not take us long to know that these were RPF soldiers. Their leader carried a two-way radio. He asked us to gather outside in the backyard and sit on the ground; we complied. Then we saw several trucks and SUVs entering the property and people getting out of them. A minute later, Paul Kagame, the leader of the rebel forces, appeared. Wearing a clean military uniform and very shiny boots, he looked at us through his round glasses with the same thin and long face we had seen in newspapers. "So you are the few survivors left!" he said, in a melancholic voice.

We all nodded respectfully, not knowing if this was a question or a comment.

"Why are they not bringing more people?" he asked, now somewhat angry. We assumed he was talking about the UN.

"If they do not have enough trucks, why are they not reaching out to us?" It was clear now that he was angry. The questions were certainly not directed to us. He seemed to be thinking out loud.

"They said they cannot allow more than thirty people in the truck," someone explained on behalf of our group.

"This is unacceptable," he said.

Kagame called some of his aides and gave them some orders.

"You can get up now," he told us. "You are no longer prisoners." His statement lingered for a long moment in our minds but did not seem to register. The notion of freedom simply did not carry its usual uplifting meaning.

Before we knew it, the convoy was gone. One by one we got up slowly, like zombies, and retreated into the large house. Throughout the day, UN trucks brought more people from the hotel. There were no smiles, no high-fives. The newly arrived settled in empty houses around the town.

One of the RPF authorities called a general meeting and began recruiting. Some men and women from our group joined the rebel army. The RPF authority asked us not to venture far from the camp, since the RPF was still fighting the Interahamwe militia. But we could go in the fields around to look for food. In the afternoon, I went out with a few other men to see what we could find.

The Kabuga area has rich soil and abundant vegetation. But the land seemed to have been abandoned. We were astounded to see no one living in the area now. The bushy land and the abundant crops in the fields were untouched, while unattended domestic animals roamed everywhere. It felt as if we had come upon a lost civilization, and we harvested what we could. We cut green bananas, caught a goat and a few chickens, and called it a day. When we got back to the house, not everybody was impressed.

"You brought the wrong kind of banana," someone said. "This is the type used to produce banana wine!"

They were right. The banana turned dark once cooked and had a sour taste. The other problem that arose was what to do with the goat and the chickens. No one had the experience or nerve to kill a live animal! A man watching us debate the whole chicken issue grabbed a large kitchen knife and headed to the backyard, visibly annoyed and mumbling something to himself. A minute later, he came back with two headless chickens in hand and literally threw them to us as if to say, What kind of men are you?

In the morning, we went back to hunt for food. This time we took someone knowledgeable in banana matters. On our way back, we passed a house half destroyed by fire. To this day, I do not know what drew me to look closely at that home. It looked like my parents' house, with a small balcony on the front and a courtyard in the back surrounded by a brick fence. I thought I saw someone sitting in the front yard, so I entered the property and what I saw made me sick. In the front of the garden, in what seemed to have been a beautiful garden, was a chair, and on the chair, a woman's body. Her hands had been tied behind the chair, and her entire body still expressed pain and agony. The upper part from the head to the chest was burnt; obviously someone had set her on fire. Although she was dead, her body seemed to command respect. Even in death she possessed a rare and noble dignity— clear enough to me but obviously not to those who killed her. The loss of such a young and beautiful life sickened me.

Christine and I were very anxious to find out who among our family members and friends had survived. Everyone among us had their own similar questions. Whenever RPF soldiers came to see us, we would press them for information. A man I knew, and a native of Christine's home region of Bugesera, now in the RPF army, told us that he was planning to head to that region to check on his own family; he promised Christine that he would bring back news of her family as well. We still did not know the extent of the killings, but we were hopeful. Nothing prepared us for the news that followed.

Two days later, the man returned. His face conveyed a gloomy expression. I could tell immediately that he brought bad news. While my heart was beating, Christine maintained a hopeful expression. But with his first words all hope was destroyed.

"Only one of your younger siblings survived," he said. Christine screamed as if stabbed in the chest. Everybody around dropped what they were doing and stared at the messenger as if he were the killer.

The man said he didn't know who the surviving sibling was. Christine, her body shaking, ran back to the house, covering her face and sobbing inconsolably. I ran after and held her as tightly as I could. She sobbed so hard that I feared she could not breathe. I wanted to console her but I could not. What possible words could I offer? All I could do was hold her in my arms and silently wait.

Christine was no stranger to loss. When she was a little girl, she lost a baby sister to illness, followed more recently by another younger sister, just six years old, and then an aunt. Each of these losses was devastating, although Christine had come to terms with her grief. But now the sorrow was unbearable.

Though we later learned that her father had survived, Christine's mother and her other six siblings had been killed. Their bodies had not been found. We would learn later that many of the victims were thrown in the Nyabarongo River, which fed into the Akagera River. On TV at the Mille Collines Hotel, we had seen images of such bodies clogging the rivers flowing into Victoria Lake in Uganda. Perhaps Christine's family members were among them.

Christine spent the following days praying and quietly meditating. As I observed her, I had so many questions about our faith. Nothing seemed to make sense. Her mother was like a saint, and she had raised her children the same way. What was God's reward for the faithful? Didn't he owe them protection and happiness? I could anticipate the typical answer: "God works in mysterious ways. . . ." But I could not be satisfied with that answer. Where was the mystery of good people being unjustly exterminated? Nothing made any sense.

20

Facing the Truth

On July 4, the RPF drove the government forces out of Kigali. We returned soon after and found a city in ruins. The air smelled of smoke and death. Many buildings showed bullet holes and smashed windows. The grass on the side of the streets had grown tall. There were few cars on the streets, mostly military vehicles. Habitable houses were scarce, and they were occupied at triple their capacity.

We almost found ourselves homeless. People I did not know had occupied my house, and they would not leave. It was near impossible for me to prove my ownership, as administrative records were in shambles. We refused to leave and ended up sleeping in the living room. Miraculously, the next morning the new occupants packed their belongings and silently slipped away. I figured they found another house.

All my furniture, the stove in the kitchen, the utensils and even pictures once hanging on the walls were missing. The content of the drawers had been emptied on the floor. Nothing of value remained in the house. Everything else I left behind, including all my pictures and my personal collection of souvenirs, had been thrown out and burned in the front yard. Nothing was left there either. People in the neighborhood and surrounding areas were taking furniture and appliances from abandoned homes. Someone offered to give us a refrigerator he had found, but we did not take it. It certainly belonged to someone else, and we did not want to steal anything. The stuff we lost did not matter at all to us. We knew we could replace them. For now, we were more concerned about finding surviving family members and planning for our life ahead.

In the days that followed I learned that my job offer at the Preferential Trade Area was no longer available. They had assumed I wasn't available and gave the job to someone else. I did nothing to pursue the matter.

Christine wanted us to try immigrating to Europe. I still had a copy of the letter of invitation sent to us while at the Mille Collines by my good friend Theopiste Butare in Geneva, Switzerland. When I found a way to call Theo, I was not prepared for what he had to tell me.

"Did you hear about what happened in Nyanza?" he asked. Until then I had no information about my hometown.

"No, I did not," I said, my anxiety already rising.

"Oh, I thought you knew," he said, apparently delaying what he had to say. I already started to fear the worst.

Theo told me that one of my coworkers at the Department of Commerce and an acquaintance of his, François Somayire, had made it to Switzerland and brought devastating news, that the entire Tutsi community and several moderate Hutu in the region of Nyanza had been decimated. That included the mayor, the teachers in the elementary and secondary schools, the judges, the priests, business leaders, workers in the public and private sector, and thousands of simple, ordinary citizens with their families. The killers hunted down men, women, and children like wild animals and exterminated them without mercy. The region as we knew it no longer existed. Even after all we had seen and heard I was filled with shock and disbelief. The Nyanza region was known for its neutrality about ethnic differences. Nyanza was the royal capital of Rwanda until the late 1950s. When the country was still a monarchy, there had never been conflicts between the two main ethnic groups, the Hutu and the Tutsi. And, while ethnic violence did erupt in different regions in the early 1960s the region of Nyanza remained unscathed. Being a native or a resident of Nyanza conveyed a sense of pride. Civility and grace were deeply embedded in the culture of the region.

I had hoped my hometown, with its reputation for tranquility, had escaped the horror of the capital. Theo paused, then spoke the words I was dreading. "I'm sorry, Bosco, but your father is among those confirmed dead."

The news took a long moment to register. I tried to say something, but I couldn't utter a sound. Tears rolled down my cheeks, and I did nothing to wipe them away. Christine and Julienne started to weep next to me, while listening to the details of that horrible story. Though my friend continued to talk, I no longer heard anything. My mind was transported back to images of my strong and respected father, and the feeling of security I always felt in his presence. I could not imagine him kneeling and begging for mercy before his killers. I felt like I had let him down. Was there not something I could have done to change his fate? My friend had no news about my mother or my younger siblings, but I became increasingly worried. What if they had met the same fate as my father?

At this point I gave up thoughts of leaving for Europe. I needed to find out who had survived and needed my help.

It was difficult to find working phones, and I couldn't drive, since my car registration was still in the hands of Paul Rusesabagina at the Mille Collines Hotel. Information was transmitted from mouth to mouth. A survivor from Bugesera told us who Christine's surviving sibling was; it was Clemence, her third younger sister. We did not know where she was at the moment. While we rejoiced over the good news, we were reminded that all of her other siblings were killed. Any good item of news was often followed by ten bad ones, unfortunately. So much more was to come.

The following day, Christine, Julienne, and I decided to walk up to the central commercial district on the Kiyovu plateau to buy food and see if we could meet people. Only a few shops were open and traffic was slow. For hours, we didn't come across a single person we knew. In that city where everyone knew everyone, it was shocking. We were now strangers in our own city. All of a sudden though, I saw a familiar face pass by. The man seemed lost in thoughts and moved like a zombie.

I startled him by calling his name, Jean. When he looked up and saw us, he came running and gave us a heartfelt hug.

"Thank God you survived! I thought I was the only one left," he said, with a weak smile on his face.

Jean Bizimana was married to my mother's cousin, Monique Kabagema. They lived with their young children close to the Institute of Statistics in Remera, a section in the eastern part of Kigali, where Monique worked as the school's administrative assistant. Though a frail man of small stature, Jean was by nature a very dynamic and lively person. Now he looked defeated, resigned. I was anxious to hear what he had to say, for my sister Chantal and her family lived on the property of the School of Statistics, and two of my younger siblings had been staying there on spring break. Judging by Jean's somber demeanor, I knew something grave had happened. I braced myself for the worst.

His eyes watered as he started telling us his story. At the beginning of the killings on April 7, his family went into hiding, but as the militia started searching all the homes in the neighborhood and killing anyone identified as Tutsi, they took refuge with many other Tutsi in the buildings of the School of Statistics. Jean was with his wife and their eight children.

Because of its international status, Jean said, the school was briefly guarded by soldiers of the UN peacekeeping mission. But after a few days the UN mission withdrew. Then government soldiers and militiamen armed with guns, machetes, and all sorts of weapons invaded the place on April 19. Here Jean paused, his voice almost choking. Then he delivered the sad news. Almost everyone there was killed, including his wife, five of his children, and my younger siblings Rose and Regis.

How much more of this could we bear? Was there to be no end to our grief? I had read stories about the Holocaust and found them beyond imagination. Now we were living the same horror, and the world still called itself "civilized." The only good news from Jean's story was that my sister Chantal, her husband Joseph, and their baby son had survived.

We hurried to go see Chantal and listened as she told us the incredible ordeal that started at the School of Statistics.

There were many people, mostly Tutsi, who took refuge within the buildings of the school and in houses occupied by its staff and faculty. The property was briefly protected by UN soldiers, who soon left, leaving the refugees unprotected. Government soldiers and Interahamwe militia then stormed the place. They forced all refugees to assemble in the main courtyard, where the Tutsi were separated from the Hutu. The Tutsi were ordered to move out of the school's property. Among them were Chantal and her baby Steve, her husband, Joseph, my younger siblings Rose and Regis, and Jean's family.

Chantal's husband, Joseph, pleaded with a soldier to save these family members. But only he and Chantal, with Steve on her back, were allowed to leave the death line. Everything happened very quickly. They desperately watched as the line started moving toward the gate of the property. Rose, Regis, and Jean's family were still on the death line. Chantal recalled that Rose was very scared and started crying, "Why are they doing this? What have we done?" The militiamen started killing the Tutsi as soon as they stepped outside the school's property, brutally chopping them with machetes, spears, and clubs. The refugees were hacked to death—men, women, and children. The militiamen kept hitting the mutilated bodies until no one was still breathing. For Chantal it was the apocalypse. It was surreal to watch the cruel execution of human beings, including her own siblings. Their bodies were then loaded on trucks and transported away. Chantal assumed they were dumped in mass graves. Had it not been for the baby on her back, she would not have found the courage to continue her fight for life.

As I listened to that horrible story and thought of the death of my little brother and sister, I felt as if my heart would explode. What was even more unbearable was the way they suffered. Their cries resonated in the back of my mind; I could hear them begging for mercy and pleading with their God for a chance to live. But the killers did not have any pity, and God did not seem to listen. Chantal continued with her story. As the situation worsened in the capital, the school's Rwandan staff and faculty were evacuated from the city toward the South. Joseph and his family took advantage of the ride. Soon they arrived in the central city of Gitarama. It had been almost a miracle to reach the city, for there were many roadblocks along the road where identity cards were checked. Joseph knew the mayor of a rural town in the region, whom he considered a friend. He rented a car and headed to the town where he left his wife and baby with relatives. He then went to see the mayor, hoping to ask for a favor and get new identity cards that would state he and his wife were Hutu. This was indeed one way a mayor could save a Tutsi during that time of chaos. What Joseph did not know, however, was that friendship was another casualty of the times. He had no way of knowing that his friend the mayor had become a monster killer.

Chantal learned from witnesses that the mayor did not even take time to listen to Joseph's plea; instead, he ordered one of his police officers to execute him on the spot.

Chantal eventually left Gitarama with her baby on her back and traveled by foot through hills and plantations. She stayed overnight at a stranger's house and left hurriedly because she heard killers were coming for her. Thank God, she reached a zone already liberated by the Rwandan Patriotic Front before anyone could hurt them.

We continued looking for family members still alive and listening to their stories. Until then we had not heard any details about Christine's family. After the evacuation from the Mille Collines Hotel, her sister Clementine had been volunteering with some other young women at a makeshift camp called the Sick Bay, caring for wounded soldiers of the RPF. She joined us as soon as she learned we were back in Kigali. She had connected with their father, Straton, and younger sister, Clemence, the only family members who survived the massacres in Bugesera. Clemence had been brought from Bugesera and started volunteering at the Sick Bay as well.

When we reconnected with Clemence we heard her story. By then we thought we had heard the most dreadful stories, but hers was far more horrendous. It shook us to the core.

The night of Wednesday, April 6, 1994, was like any other night for Clemence with her family in Bugesera—quiet and peaceful. Except for Christine and Clementine living in the capital, all her other five siblings and a young cousin living with them were home. It was school vacation, and the children were relaxed, enjoying a hassle-free time with their parents. Everyone was excited for an upcoming wedding in the family. They said their prayers and all went to bed unconcerned, looking forward for another wonderful day.

The family learned of the president's death on the radio the next morning. Very soon the area was under attack. It was soon confirmed that local mobs known to be members of the Interahamwe militia were attacking homes of Tutsi. People were screaming and leaving their homes. Very quickly the situation became chaotic. Houses were burned down and people were hunted like animals. Clemence and the rest of her family left their home and took refuge at a local elementary school, where hundreds of other people, mostly Tutsi, had already gathered. Throughout the day more people arrived, including many wounded. Soon the number was in the thousands.

A group of men and teenagers among the refugees started organizing a resistance at the elementary school. When the militia attacked they were ready. They threw stones and fought with sticks. For several days, they prevailed over the assailants, although they suffered some casualties. Attacks came only during the day. Militiamen took a break at night, which allowed people to go back to their homes in the evening or stay with friends. Clemence and her family stayed with one of her cousins in a nearby house. They were hopeful that someone would soon come to their rescue and end the violence.

As days went by, though, the attacks multiplied and became deadlier. The local militia was reinforced by government soldiers and hundreds more militiamen who came from the capital, equipped with guns, machetes, and other sorts of weapons. Brave men, women, and children fought as they could, but their resistance was quickly destroyed. Those who were able, ran; those who couldn't, died. Many were literally decapitated.

This was not the end of Clemence's story. In fact, it was only the beginning. Clemence's mother called her children and gave each

of them a rosary. She told them to be brave and to pray. Clemence
did not know this was their last moment together. All around people were running for their lives. Men, women, children. Hundreds
ran toward the small church of Ntarama, others to the surrounding hills and valleys. Clemence and her family ran toward the
church, but they found it full, overflowing with hundreds of people.
They ran at random, and soon got separated. Some went north and
others went south.

Clemence and her older brother Murenzi stayed together and
hid in the woods in the surrounding hills. Eventually Murenzi, who
was with his girlfriend, thought of a plan for them to head south
and cross into Burundi, which was about thirty kilometers away.
When the opportunity arose, the three of them left and walked
the entire night. But at dawn, they found they had been walking in
circles and did not get far. The next day they were to try again, but
an attack came and they were separated.

In the chaos Clemence met an old classmate, also Tutsi, whose
brother lived nearby with his wife and three children. For several
days, she stayed with them; they would all hide during the day and
come back home at night when the Interahamwe were gone. The
woman of the house was pregnant and sick. Clemence would help
the couple take care of their infant daughter and would take her
into hiding whenever there was an attack. As days went by, the
woman got sicker. Unfortunately, there was no way to take her to a
medical facility. Helplessly her family and Clemence watched her
die; they buried her in the backyard.

There was no time for grief, as the family was always on the run.
Shortly after, the death squads launched their biggest and deadli-
est attack ever. Hundreds of Tutsi hiding in the ceilings of their
homes, in the houses of their Hutu neighbors, or in the woods and
bushes of the surrounding hills were discovered and slaughtered
like animals. Again, survivors ran for their lives. Clemence and
her friends ran with the flow of hundreds of other people fleeing,
with no destination in mind. Unexpectedly they found themselves
at the edge of a vast swamp that extends along the Akagera River;
without hesitation, they ran into it. They progressed deep into the

swamp's wetland and hid in the tall and thick papyrus bushes. More people continued to come, and soon they were in the thousands. Clemence found her older sister Claire among the swamp's refugees.

For a brief period of time the swamp was all quiet. People were too terrified to make any sound; even the moaning of the wounded had stopped. Clemence quietly stood in the bushes and prayed. If only God could keep the killers away. The nightmare resumed as death squads arrived and started killing people hiding at the edges of the swamp. Some of the men fought back, but they were outnumbered. The militiamen killed without mercy, all day long. Hundreds of men, women and children were hacked to death. Deep inside the swamp, thousands of refugees helplessly listened to the screams and agony of the unfortunate victims. Once again, Clemence turned to God, praying that her turn would not arrive.

As the evening sun went down, the horrible massacres stopped temporarily. The killers did not bother attacking at night. The carnage was only a daytime "job." Clearly the Interahamwe were confident their victims had no way out, and they seemed to know no rescuers would come. Every morning they came in columns, chanting, whistling, and beating drums. "God has delivered them," the militiamen chanted. To find their victims they were guided by the cries of babies, and they cut the bushes with machetes to discover those hiding within. For days and weeks, the swamp refugees lived in terror, knowing it was only a matter of time before death would strike. Only nighttime provided some respite from death. Late at night the refugees would sneak out of their hiding places and go dig sweet potatoes and other root vegetables in the fields. It was extremely risky but they had no other choice. They ate the food raw.

One morning the attacks stopped coming. The only sounds came from the injured. Soon some refugees started emerging from their hiding places. They learned that soldiers of the RPF were stationed nearby and that the Interahamwe were fleeing. The news spread across the swamp among the few remaining survivors. As they cautiously emerged, they witnessed the most horrible picture imaginable. There were dead bodies everywhere, thousands of them, stiffened in agony. There were many injured, covered in blood, still fighting for their lives. Clemence discovered that Claire was among them.

Up to this point, Clemence had surprised us with her calm delivery. But when she started talking about her sister Claire, she struggled to regain her composure and burst into tears. Understandably so. She discovered that Claire's entire body was marked with deep machete cuts and covered in blood. Her limbs had been butchered and her feet were nearly severed. All around people were running. Someone shouted that everyone should evacuate immediately, as the area was still dangerous; they would have to come back for the wounded. Clemence couldn't lift her sister alone. She promised she would come back soon with help, then took off. As she ran uphill, she often looked back to where her sister lay, bleeding to death. The look on Claire's face would never leave her; a look of pain, hopelessness, and unbearable sadness.

The surrounding hills north and east of the swamp were already in the hands of the RPF rebels. As soon as the swamp survivors reached the top of the hill, they were efficiently escorted to a safe zone, which they were not allowed to leave. Though they pleaded with the rebels to evacuate the wounded from the swamp, they were reminded that this remained a combat zone. Clemence remained hopeful. Soon enough some of the injured were indeed brought from the swamp, but Claire was not among them. Hours turned into days and days turned into weeks. She knew her sister had not made it. No one could survive in that condition. With everything she had been through in the past several weeks, the most excruciating feeling for Clemence was the tragic end of her sibling. She felt responsible and blamed herself.

Clemence kept her tears silent, aware that among her fellow survivors there were many who had suffered even more. Fresh information on more massacres in the region were emerging every day. The stories were horrifying. The swamp survivors learned of the fate that met those family members who took refuge at the Ntarama and Nyamata Catholic churches. They had fled to the churches in hopes that no one would touch them in the house of

God. Almost all of them were savagely killed. Clemence got word from survivors who knew her family that her mother, her younger sister, and her two younger brothers were among hundreds of people who fled toward Kigali, hoping to cross the Nyabarongo valley and reach Rebero, one of the steep hills that surround the capital and was already under control of the RPF. Unfortunately, as we had already learned, they were ambushed and killed by Interahamwe and government soldiers at the Nyabarongo River, a few miles before reaching the Rebero hill. The last piece of devastating news for Clemence came from a young man who witnessed the last moments of her brother Murenzi, who was brutally murdered with his girlfriend after he knocked at the door of a convent that he thought still housed Catholic nuns. Instead they were met by bloodthirsty local youths of the Interahamwe militia who had taken over the convent. As for the young man who witnessed their brutal murder, he ran and threw himself in thick shrubs that bordered the property. The killers looked for him for hours but finally gave up. He survived to tell the story.

For so long I had thought of our world as an oasis of life; not perfect, but nevertheless a place of love and kindness. Now I was confronted with the ugly reality. I saw a world of hatred and savagery. I was now fearful of its people—heartless and cruel for the most part, careless or indifferent at best. I lost the capacity for hope. Where could I possibly find it? For a while, after listening to Clemence's story, no one could speak. Christine had not stopped crying. Every detail was like a direct stab in her heart. She was gasping so hard that I was afraid her tears would choke her. But these tears would eventually dry out. I was more concerned about the tears of her soul. I could only hope time would help her and her surviving sisters heal.

Meanwhile, I remained anxious to learn about my mother's fate. I retrieved my car from the Mille Collines parking lot and my registration from Paul, who was now back at the hotel, then drove south the next day with Christine, Chantal, and Julienne to my hometown of Nyanza. We arrived late in the morning. The town was deserted. It looked like towns I had seen in Western movies. The few people I passed were strangers to me. The gaping doors and windows of my parents' house clearly told me my mother could not be around. It was quiet. Not a living soul was stirring. The household furniture was missing. All the rooms were completely empty, except for papers and a few of my father's books covering the floor. In a corner stood the statue of the Virgin Mary that my mother had brought from Kibeho, a shrine in the South of the country associated with several apparitions of the Mother of Jesus. I picked up the statue and held it tightly against my chest.

Julienne found on the floor a photo album that contained several pictures of our younger sister Rose. The pictures were recent. They showed a radiant Rose posing with some of her high school friends or alone in a beautiful garden, probably at her school. That was typical of Rose; full of joy and life. Tears flowed down my cheeks as I flipped through the album and saw again her glowing smile. I missed her terribly. I looked around for more pictures but saw none, including the framed photo of my parents on their wedding day, standing in front of the church. In that photo, they were well dressed and handsome. Next to them was my uncle Hildegarde, wearing a bow tie. The picture was a treasure to me; it had been hanging in my parents' living room since before I was born. Now it was gone, forever. I was stunned to see how the killers seemed to have erased all traces of life from the home. Of all that remained, I put the statue of the Virgin Mary and Rose's album in my car, and we headed toward the commercial district.

My father's pharmacy was situated on the main street entering the city. This usually busy area of town was now quiet and free of traffic. We did not know the few people we crossed on the road; they seemed like distant and cold strangers to us; no one would make eye contact, as if to avoid embarrassing questions. The door of my father's pharmacy was open, and not surprisingly, it was empty. Even the shelves were gone. Outside we saw a woman coming toward us. As she got closer I recognized her. Her husband, Bahore, owned the store across the street. A good friend of my mother, Mrs. Bahore was among a few Tutsi people who survived. She gave me a long and warm hug, then began to cry. From her tears I immediately knew that my mother did not make it. I dreaded to hear the details. Nevertheless, I accepted her invitation to share a soda in her store. Once we settled down, she started telling us a story that I knew would haunt me for the rest of my life.

The killings started in Nyanza after April 20, just after the interim president had visited the southern city of Butare and delivered a racially charged, incendiary speech. The Nyanza region, with its history of conciliatory relations between Hutus and Tutsis, posed a challenge to the regime's divisionist policies. The genocidal strategists brought into the region militiamen and soldiers to carry out their plan. They first killed the mayor, a moderate Hutu, attaching his body to a pickup truck and dragging him through the streets. As the security of the region deteriorated, my parents decided to move out of town and stay with my father's uncle several miles away in the rural hills, while waiting for things to settle down. They told the family aide, Makongo, where they were headed. Makongo was a Hutu, but for my parents he was just another member of our family. They had total confidence in him and asked him to come tell them when the violence was over. Before they left, my father took some money from his pharmacy business, then he and my mother left the city on foot, walking several miles in the hills and valleys to their hiding place. Other family members on my father's side were hiding there as well.

A week later, on April 26, Makongo paid them a visit. But he was not alone. Several dozen local militiamen, armed with machetes and clubs, were with him. The militiamen rushed into the house and immediately killed my father's uncle Enoch, his wife, Verediane, their son David, and my father's younger brother. One of my cousins escaped through a window and ran. The Interahamwe took both my parents to bring them to the leader of the regional militia. My parents were the big fishes who could not be killed unceremoniously. The militiamen ordered my father and my mother to walk several miles across the hills, surrounded by an army of militiamen that now included Makongo and several peasants of the surrounding hills. They began chanting victory songs, constantly threatening my parents with their machetes.

The leader of the militia was a man named Karege, a ferocious person who prided himself on having orchestrated the killing of hundreds of Tutsi people in a matter of days. He was stationed at the Kavumu roadblock, situated at the intersection of the paved road leading to the southern city of Butare and the road leading to Nyanza. As soon my parents got there, they bound my father to a tree, and they ordered my mother to sit down on the side of the road. Knowing my mother was not going to be safe, my father tried to negotiate, begging the militia chief to spare her life. He offered all the money he had earned at his pharmacy The militiaman took the money, but offered nothing in return.

My father begged the militiamen not to kill my mother. These were the last words he was heard saying. The militia chief did not respond. Instead, late on the morning of April 26, 1994, he aimed his gun and fired a single shot to my father's head. On the side of the road there were women whose husbands had been killed and who were awaiting their turn. Instantly they all screamed. My mother pulled a rosary from her bag, and all the women started praying with her. Moments later a pickup truck came and my father's body was taken to one of the numerous mass graves in the city of Nyanza.

The militia chief did not know what to do with the women. At that time orders to kill women and children had not yet arrived. Minutes later a car pulled up. Its occupants briefly spoke with the militia leader then left. My mother was taken to the house of a man who owned a restaurant in town and who lived nearby. The other women were taken as well to different places in the area. My mother and these women may have believed that their lives were spared. But three days later, on April 29, militiamen took my mother and these other women to a house in Kavumu, a locality near the town on Nyanza. They tied their hands and feet and packed them into a small room. They then threw several grenades in the room through its tiny window, stood back and watched. The explosions were heard in the entire locality. After a little while, the militiamen collected the bodies and threw them into nearby latrines.

I listened to this story with disbelief. My parents had always worked hard and sacrificed so much for the well-being of the community. They saved many lives during their medical careers, and they worked long hours every day, often covering emergencies at night. They had always been first responders. They did not work for any reward or personal gain. In fact, they lived paycheck to paycheck, barely covering the numerous needs of their seven children. They worked tirelessly for the people of the region without discrimination. I found it hard to believe that the same people they had served either participated in their killing or looked the other way.

I would have paid anything to know where their bodies had been buried. There was no way to know, I was told. Only their killers, and maybe bystanders, would know. Unfortunately, all of them had fled. They had crossed the border into Congo as the South of Rwanda fell into the hands of the RPF army. Maybe Makongo was among them. I wished I could see him again, ask him questions and understand his motivations. I heard he was recruited by the militia when my parents went into hiding. The killers needed him to know where my parents were. Technically he was on the militiamen's side. But I did not hear anyone accuse him of participating in the killings. Looking back, I did not recall any wrongdoing he ever did. My mind was instead filled with good memories. We played soccer together, traveled to my grandmother's place together; he taught me how to whistle, and how to ride a bike. We gave each other rides in a wheelbarrow. He had been a big brother to me when I was younger. In some way, he was a victim of the system, a system that put him in an ethnic category and held him its prisoner. Maybe someday, somehow, I thought, our paths would cross again. If they did, I hoped to do my best to free him from the cage of guilt in which he surely held himself captive.

I did not stay in my hometown for the night. There was no place to stay, and I had no desire to stay. We drove next to Butare, where Christine's aunt, Sister Teya, lived with her community of the Little Sisters of Jesus.

21

An Intellectual City out of Its Mind

Butare was the home of the National University and other important institutions. It was a happy and peaceful place to live, and everyone associated in any way with Butare was proud. Now we wondered what the city looked like and if it had maintained its calm.

Teya and the other Little Sisters of Jesus welcomed us with open arms and long hugs. The Little Sisters are a congregation inspired by the French desert hermit Charles de Foucauld, who lived in North Africa in the early twentieth century. They live a contemplative life among the poor, imitating the "hidden life" of Jesus in the years he spent as a carpenter in Nazareth and helping the most vulnerable members of the community. Their large brick house, situated half a mile from the Butare commercial district, did not give a hint whether violence had hit the home. Everything seemed to be in place. It was only when the nuns started telling their story that we understood the depth of the tragedy they experienced. For several hours, Teya told us a story that shook us to the core.

When the killings started on April 7, Teya stayed in the house with fourteen other Little Sisters: seven Tutsis and seven Hutus. The Sisters helped many people hide at their large house. Some were in the ceiling. Most came at night after climbing the fence of the property. The nuns initially thought that the killings were going to last maybe only one week or two. Instead, they lasted three months: "a hundred days of horror, of torture, of wickedness," Teya said.

138

Sister Teya (left) and the Little Sisters of Jesus who survived the genocide.

"On Tuesday, April 19, 1994, interim president Theodore Sindikubwabo arrived in Butare and delivered an incendiary speech, in which he incited citizens to kill their Tutsi neighbors," Teya recalled. "After that speech, soldiers and militiamen arrived at our house. They killed six very young people. The youngest was twelve years old, and the others were between twenty-one and twenty-six. The killers smashed these young people's heads with stones. We could hear their screams and agony."

My entire body wanted to scream as I listened to this story. But I kept quiet.

"Then soldiers caught a young Tutsi man who tried to run as they approached," Teya continued. "They accused the young man of trying to reach for one of the soldiers' guns, but this was not true. They simply wanted a reason to kill him. They forced us to assemble in the courtyard of our house and watch them beat the young man to death. Then they started striking him repeatedly with large sticks of wood taken from firewood bundles we kept behind the house. I closed my eyes and covered my ears as the young man was screaming, covered in blood. The soldiers continued to hit him until he died."

I could feel the pain in Teya's voice, going through the details of this horrifying story. Again, I couldn't believe what I was hearing.

Among others hiding in the house was Teya's nephew, Renee Kayijamahe, who miraculously had been able to get out of Kigali and reach Butare. "He was also executed by one of the soldiers," Teya told us.

"This soldier then ordered us to pour him some water to wash off the blood of the 'cockroach' he had just killed. I thought my heart was going to explode, thinking this man had just killed my nephew and was bragging about it."

"I cannot explain the sentiment I felt at that moment," Teya added. "It was a sentiment of helplessness and sadness—sadness that eats you up deep inside, truly. I had never had that sentiment before. The only thing that helped me was to think that our God, who took a human face and was called Jesus, went through the same anguish of death; this helped me live. I felt that I was not alone, because Jesus passed through that path. He knows what it feels like."

Christine and I listened intently, thinking of these innocent young victims, including her cousin Renee, killed so brutally and horribly. We looked at Teya and the rest of the Little Sisters, wondering how they could endure the horror they witnessed. Despite the depth of their sorrow, they were serene, very much at peace.

The nuns did not know what to do with the bodies of these young victims. The only people Teya thought of who could help were prisoners. She had been frequenting prisons for several years to read the Bible with the inmates and she knew the director. She contacted him for help.

"The director sent in some prisoners, and they hastily buried the bodies," she told us. "When they were leaving, I heard one of them saying, 'This young lady we buried was still breathing,'" Teya recalled.

"It never occurred to me that anyone who was buried that day could really be alive," Teya said. "Two days later, in the evening, I heard someone knocking on the door, but it was not the usual knock; it was different; it was a weak knock. We came and asked who this was. We heard a woman's voice, saying, 'It's Jeanne.' It was unbelievable! Jeanne was one of the people that the prisoners buried. I opened the door and immediately called another Sister who was a nurse. Jeanne looked at us, and we saw that she recognized us; then she fell into a coma."

"I think she felt secure now, after fighting for her life for the last three days," Teya continued. "She was in a state I had never seen before; between life and death. When we asked her something she responded, but we could see the conversation did not really register in her mind. We took her in our house. She was deeply wounded; a bayonet had pierced her head. Her eye socket was very damaged, and we were afraid her eye was destroyed, but it was still in place. Her head and other parts of her body had been smashed with stones."

"My God, what a story!" Christine whispered to me with a heavy sigh.

In the morning, some among the Hutu sisters took Jeanne to the hospital, but on the way they came across militiamen. Whenever militiamen saw a wounded person, they knew it was a Tutsi. The Sisters decided to bring Jeanne back home. She had so many wounds, but there was no medication at the house. "We treated her with boiled water only, clean water," Teya said.*

That was not the end of the Sisters' story. The following day, militiamen came with machetes, clubs, and spears to attack them, accusing the nuns of hiding "cockroaches." Teya called a Hutu friend to inform him about the situation, and he gave her a phone number to call for help. When she called, the man at the end of the line told her in a menacing tone, "I'm going to come and exterminate all of you. I know you are hiding Father Modeste; I will destroy everything in your house."

Teya was startled by the threat. Modeste Mungwarareba, a well-known Catholic priest in the city of Butare, was indeed hiding

---

* An amazing update on this story: Today Jeanne has finished her studies at the National University of Rwanda. Every year on May 17, the day of remembrance, she is always there to help the Little Sisters of Jesus and pray with them. Teya says there is something peaceful in her, a kind of spiritual balance. Everyone around her feels like she experienced a moment marked by the presence of the Lord. She talks much of seeing "the other" as a brother or sister, whoever they are.

in the ceiling of the nuns' house. Teya wondered how this man knew. She was certain the nuns had kept the secret.

"We do not have Father Modeste," Teya lied, hoping she sounded convincing.

"Are you certain?" the man asked. Teya immediately felt the man was trying to trick her.

"I'm certain; he is not here," she said firmly. But then she got very scared. If there was a search and Father Modeste was found, no one in the house would survive.

But the man was evidently satisfied with Teya's answer. He must have been a high-ranking officer in the army because shortly after, soldiers came to help the nuns. When they arrived, militiamen were already in the kitchen, ready to enter the rooms and start their search. Teya recalled the quick prayer she said at that moment: "Lord Jesus, help us; show us that you are with us." But the soldiers forced the militiamen out of the property.

Toward the end of June, someone told the nuns that a meeting had taken place at the military camp where it was decided to exterminate all Tutsi in the religious mission in the Butare diocese, starting with the bishop's residence and the seminary. As Teya recalled, "I felt that kind of fear that burns your insides. I couldn't focus; the prospect of death was unbearable."

But to the nuns' relief, the killers did not come. It turned out that the Rwandan Patriotic Front was fast approaching and that a French-led military operation was also underway. The two forces had agreed to a cease-fire, with a specific time frame, making it possible for people to leave Butare and go to an area in southwestern Rwanda secured by the French. Soon the nuns learned that convoys of civilians were leaving the city, escorted by French troops. Many people in the city left, including some of the nuns, but Teya decided to stay. She was afraid she could still be killed at a roadblock outside the city. "If I were to die, I preferred dying in our house," Teya said.

Teya recalled that on July 1 the whole day and night and into the following day the air was filled with the sound of combat. Clearly this was a battle between two armies. The nuns thought the fighting was between the RPF and the last bastion of government forces and Interahamwe militia, unwilling to admit defeat.

"Then it was total silence; the silence of death." News spread that the Patriotic Front now occupied Butare and that they had also captured Kigali. Three days later, on July 4, the end of the war was declared on national radio.

The ordeal was over for the Little Sisters of Jesus and for at least thirty other people hiding in their house, including Father Modeste, who never left the ceiling until the war was over. But the return to calm was nothing to celebrate.

"I fell into a very desolate situation," said Teya. "I learned that I no longer had a family; I had lost friends, coworkers and neighbors. It was a complete social emptiness. I felt dizzy, going through names and learning that this one has been killed, and that one was dead as well. . . . The impression that Rwanda had become a land of desolation, a land of death, was disturbing. Even the birds, which I like a lot, were feasting on the human flesh in the hills. Rwanda had become a vast graveyard."

"I was pained to see that Rwanda had reached the bottom," Teya continued. "One could not go lower. I did not stop asking myself what the future now held for this country. When you reach the bottom, you can stay there and die, or choose to go back up. I prayed that we do the latter, that we surrender our hearts and souls to God. I was comforted thinking that wherever death can take us, even deep under, the Lord is there. He preceded us there, to pull us back up. Only God is capable of pulling life from death. It's a face of God that I happened to discover, that I met in my prayers and meditation: the face of a God who stays with us, even in the depth of human miseries."

Teya told us that after the genocide she visited some survivors, most of whom were widows and small children; she seemed very concerned about their well- being.

"These poor people were lost and disoriented, and I totally understood their feelings," Teya said. "I recall at some point wondering: If I do not die, how am I going to live? I felt I couldn't live other than like someone who was given a second life—a life that escaped from the grave. I know that for many survivors life can represent emptiness, isolation, and hopelessness. But I always think there is a side of that life that contrasts with death, that is like the life the Lord drew out of the tomb. It's a new life of building hope in others—a life that should be offered completely, in total humility."

I looked at Teya and saw in her the expression of hope, grace, and intelligence. She spoke with assurance and optimism even though the time called for desolation. I had always known Teya as a warm and affectionate person, but I had never discovered the depth of her thinking and the strength of her faith. That very moment was inspirational for me, a rare bright moment in these times of despair.

While in Butare, I asked around to know about the fate of my mother's uncle, Theophile Sebalinda, the man who spoke on behalf of my family during my engagement ceremony to Christine. He was a well-known veterinarian in Butare, highly regarded by everyone around him, mainly for his wisdom, knowledge, and eloquence. Everything about him commanded respect—his character, his demeanor, his physical stature. Yet, he was a humble and generous man, a gentle giant, known for his kindness and strong Catholic faith.

I quickly learned the heartbreaking, painful truth. Sebalinda was unfortunately among the first people to be killed in the city; he died along with almost everyone in his beautiful family, including his lovely wife, Immaculee, his three sons, his two daughters and their husbands, and his two little grandchildren.

I left Butare with a numb feeling. It was a place my family lived until I was eight years old. I had fond memories of the city, of its cathedral, its museum, its effervescent commercial district, its neon lights, and, most importantly, its kind people. It was known as the intellectual capital of the country. Now it had become the city of death. I couldn't fathom how this happened; I left the place with a sense of confusion and profound loss.

As we drove away from Butare, Christine, Chantal, Julienne, and I were mostly silent, reflecting on the horrifying stories we had heard in the past few days. As if to distract from the pain,

Christine and Julienne started flipping through the album found at my parents' house containing pictures of my sister Rose with some of her high school friends. It was the only souvenir that connected us to a deceased family member. I found it precious.

On our way, we picked up a soldier of the RPF who was looking for a ride to Kigali. He was young and thin. He looked like my younger brother Jean Paul, who had joined the RPF in the first months of the struggle. My parents had sent him to neighboring Burundi to attend high school because of the lack of opportunities for Tutsi in Rwanda, but he interrupted his education, feeling the need to answer the RPF's call. Every feature of this young man now reminded me of my brother. Giving him a ride was the least I could do.

But soon we realized the young soldier was in an irritable mood and somewhat aggressive. Occasionally he had outbursts of anger. He would point his gun in a ready to shoot position and we would brace for trouble. We only had some respite when he noticed the album. He grabbed it, and for the rest of the trip he was occupied flipping through its pages. He told us he loved it and wanted to keep it. We thought it was a joke. But when we arrived in Kigali, he insisted the album should be his. We chose not to argue. Maybe he was dealing with some sort of traumatic condition. He took the album, opened the door, and disappeared in the sea of pedestrians. We never saw the precious photo album again. We had just witnessed another side of the Rwandan tragedy.

22

Nothing Makes Sense Anymore

Back in Kigali we again began looking for any family members and friends who might have survived. Searching for survivors had become an almost full-time job. I still had to hear about uncles, aunts, cousins, friends, and coworkers. Communication was not easy, as the phone lines in the city were still not working. Also, people had been displaced due to the destruction and the lingering insecurity, and one needed to move around carefully because of land mines. It was hard to know who survived and who did not. But by word of mouth, the truth came out gradually. The stories were always horrible, and the details unforgiving. They offered no answers, no comfort, no assurance—just the ugly, brutal truth.

No one I was looking for survived. It was beyond shocking. The list included my paternal aunts, Epiphanie, a hospital worker, and Iphigenie, a civil servant for the interior ministry. Iphigenie had boarded a minibus toward the South with her three boys and her daughter. At a roadblock she was ordered to get out of the car with her children. She said she had no children. Though the children were very young, they were smart enough not to follow or make eye contact with their mother. The minibus left her at the roadblock. She was killed, but her quick thinking saved her children.

My cousin and roommate Philippe, who taught math in high school in Kigali, my maternal uncle Hildegarde, an elementary school teacher, and his son, my godfather Aimable Kagirigiri along his wife, his three daughters, his son-in-law, and his baby granddaughter were among the dead. My closest friends, my Tutsi coworkers—none of them survived. The list of victims was too long to recount. The same was true for Christine.

Additionally, the list of victims included my very good friends Constantin Cyubahiro, Aloys Niyoyita, and Godefroid Ritararenga, whose presence at my engagement celebration had contributed to the joyous occasion. For several years, I had been blessed to have these men, together with my brother-in-law, Joseph, around me. In them I had complete trust; I knew I could count on each of them, anytime. And I knew they felt the same way about me. They were like brothers to me. Now they were gone, leaving behind dreams cut short by unfortunate destiny. Miraculously, their widows and children survived. It was a rare bright spot in a very darkened sky.

Christine had been looking for information about her uncle, Laurent Kayijamahe, and his five daughters and two sons with whom she lived for six years while attending high school in Kigali. For several days Christine couldn't get any information. As she started having some hope of finding them alive, the sad news came. We learned the entire family was killed in the last week of June, just one week before the liberation of Kigali. The circumstances of their death were not clear to us. We heard soldiers came to the home with a vehicle and took Laurent and his six children, supposedly to bring them to safety at the Sainte Famille Church located in the heart of the capital. Unfortunately, there was a roadblock down the hill from the house, manned by dozens of militiamen. Laurent and his children were reportedly stripped of their clothes and killed on the spot.

With all the losses, I felt like the killers had severed the ties with most of the people in my life and had taken away my future. Without them, I knew life was not going to be the same anymore. Christine and I started counting the dead. In total, there were ninety-seven victims from both our families. Including friends and our closest acquaintances, the number increased substantially. Of all the people who had attended our engagement ceremony months earlier, only a handful had survived.

People discovered mass graves everywhere, every day. Only a few of the victims could be identified, either because of their clothing or, in rare cases, because of the testimonies of the killers and bystanders. Looking for loved ones became a permanent job for survivors.

There were no clear statistics just after the genocide, but early estimates placed the number of victims at nearly one million people, including three hundred thousand children. Entire families had been completely wiped out. Almost all property belonging to the victims had been destroyed. Many survivors lost limbs, and their bodies showed deep physical scars. Some were still in pain. I had never imagined I would see such horrific images. Many women had lost not only their spouses but also their children. Among them, many were raped or subjected to other forms of sexual violence.

The psychological impact was incalculable. For the first time, I heard of the word "trauma." In fact, a large number of survivors suffered from post-traumatic stress disorder and from chronic traumatic grief. There was no adequate counseling structure after the genocide to help survivors suffering from these conditions. The few organizations that tried to help in that area did not have trained personnel to deal with the issue. Consequently, survivors did not get any help or simply received inadequate counseling that did not heal their psychological wounds.

At the same time Rwanda was dealing with another big problem. With the advance of the rebels of the RPF, soldiers of the defeated government forces, politicians of the genocidaires' regime, and members of the Interahamwe militia fled toward neighboring Congo, threatening the fragile return to calm inside Rwanda. It was clear to anyone that the conflict was not over yet. Also, millions of Hutu civilians, many of whom did not participate in the genocide, also fled to Congo. Many parts of Rwanda's countryside were almost empty. Meanwhile, the refugee situation in eastern Congo was quickly becoming a humanitarian crisis.

Little by little, as the first light of peace and security dawned again, former refugees repopulated the country. They felt grateful to come back to Rwanda and have a land to call home. Most of these did not live through the genocide but came after it was over. These included relatives we had never met or had not seen for decades. My brother Aimable returned from Burundi and lived with us. He would never again see the parents who had sent him abroad as a teenager to enjoy educational opportunities. He would never have the chance to see again the siblings he had left at a very young age. But he was back, safe and sound. That's all that counted.

Returnees included members of the Rwandan Patriotic Front. I had been looking for my little brother Jean Paul. I was very anxious to find him. The last time we saw each other he was about to finish high school but still looked like a baby to me. Hopefully, he was back now, I thought.

The truth came from one of my cousins, a soldier in the RPF army. He said my brother did not make it. He was shot and died shortly after he joined the RPF. My cousin started describing how Jean Paul died from his wounds after several days of suffering, with no appropriate medical care available; but I stopped him short. I had no desire to hear the details.

The emptiness surrounding us was almost unbearable. How does one live with the enormity of evil and remain a sane human being? Family members and many friends were dead, while neighbors and other friends had fled. Sometimes I felt numb and isolated, and Christine would tell me she felt the same way. More painful was the fact that we had not had the chance of mourning our family members. Their bodies had been buried in mass graves or thrown into rivers. I now realized the importance of grieving and mourning a loved one. We needed a place to go and occasionally deposit flowers in loving memory of our families. We started asking if anyone knew where the bodies of our family members had been buried. We did not have many responses.

But eventually someone in my hometown decided to talk. He knew how my mother and several other women were killed and where their bodies had been buried. He told a friend of my family who called us. When my family and I arrived in Nyanza the next day, the exhumation of the bodies had already been done. Other families were there as well to identify their loved ones. It was not an easy task since the bodies were not recognizable. There was a shocking detail that didn't escape anyone at the scene that day:

the victims' legs and hands had been tied up with rope. It was
not easy to put a name on each body. I was starting to despair
when the woman who had called us pointed to one of the bodies
and said:

"This is Febronie; I recognize the sweater she was wearing."
That was enough for me. There was another detail that helped
eliminate any doubt. A rosary was found in her right hand.

"I know she had been praying, and she always had her rosary,"
the woman said. I knew this was true. I was now sure this was my
mother's body. The body was put in a casket, then taken to a cha-
pel at the Nyanza church, where we started a wake.

Later that day, I allowed myself to have a quiet moment with
the person who had brought me into this world and had loved me
unconditionally. I stood next to the casket and spoke to her. As I
did so, I burst into tears. My words were that of a lost child, confused, fragile, and lonely. I told her I was sorry. She had always
been there for me, but I had not. I had promised myself to take
care of her someday, to make her happy; now it was too late. My
intentions were now useless, as if they had never existed.

The wake lasted a couple of days; family members, most of whom
consisted of my mother's sisters and brothers who had recently
returned from exile in Burundi, sat quietly around the casket,
keeping company with the sister they had hoped to be reunited
with after more than thirty years of separation. The few survivors
from the town stopped by to pay their respect and show support.
The wake was a special moment for survivors, most of whom were
not able to find the bodies of their loved ones. This wake became
theirs; we mourned together and we grieved together. The church
service and the funeral followed in my hometown. My mother was
buried in the backyard of my parents' house.

"Does life actually have any meaning?" Christine asked me as
we drove away from Nyanza. I pondered the question and struggled to find a good answer. All my life such a question had never
crossed my mind.

"It's hard to find any meaning to life right now," I finally
responded, contradicting my usual sense of optimism. But that
was the best I could say.

I hated waking up in the morning. The excitement of a new day did not exist anymore. Reality was cruel, unforgiving. Every day my pain intensified. It was the pain of the soul—burning, intense, and persistent. Nothing I had believed made sense anymore. Trust, hope, faith were now empty words. No doubt, life had lost its meaning.

Ever since I was a child, nothing was more gratifying than the feeling that I was part of a strong and good family, known for its integrity and honor. Other friends, family members, and neighbors had added pride and purpose to my existence. They included teachers, members of the clergy, public servants, small business owners, or simply farmers. They were all decent, hardworking people, defined by integrity and common decency. My engagement to Christine had even extended the family further and introduced me to more people with admirable qualities.

My motivation, my sense of happiness and well-being had derived from belonging to a community that shared common values, interests, and aspirations. Now everyone I had looked up to was dead. My world had turned upside down. The comfort I drew from belonging to a strong community had dissipated.

After several weeks, I was still looking for words to express my pain. Sometimes I wondered if I had just had a bad dream. How could this be? At times, my mind simply couldn't grasp the possibility of a complete annihilation of the world that encircled me. It was as though my brain occasionally turned on a protective instinct of disbelief and denial just to keep me hoping and going. But this defensive impulse was surreal; it was vapor, a thin layer on the surface of my subconscious. Deep inside was the open awareness that projected its full light on the reality I had to deal with. The complete annihilation was real.

The realization of reality made me angry. I was angry at this land that produced so many criminals and sowed so much hatred and discord. I was angry at its leaders and soldiers to whom we had entrusted our safety and well-being, only for them to betray us. I was angry at many of my fellow citizens for their active involvement in the slaughter, and at those who lacked the courage to intervene. The masterminds of the genocide had relied not only on the zealous participants but on the silent bystanders and those who looked the other way. It was not surprising to see reckless politicians sow chaos and desolation for their own gain. What was more troubling for me was to see regular people acquire bestial instincts and line up in large numbers to commit horrible crimes. I later learned of words of Primo Levi, a survivor of Auschwitz: "Monsters exist, but they are too few in number to be truly dangerous. More dangerous are the common men, the functionaries ready to believe and to act without asking questions."

I was angry at the world for standing by again and watching, and at the United Nations and their useless "blue helmets." It had been reported that UN officials in New York were made aware, way before the start of the killings in Rwanda, of the plan to massacre at least ten thousand people a day, but they chose not to act! After the killings started, the UN even decided to pull out most of its troops, leaving innocent men, women, and children at the mercy of bloodthirsty mobs. European nations sent troops to protect and evacuate only their own citizens. The United States sent a couple hundred Marines, who waited in the neighboring Burundi but never intervened.

At the concentration camp in Dachau, there is a memorial that says, "Never Again." I began to wonder, "Had humanity not learned anything from the horrors of the Holocaust, from the ethnic cleansing less than a half a century ago?"

And here it was happening again, right before my eyes. And I was in the midst of it! What is it that makes us forget our past and condemns us to repeat the same evils of previous generations? Did the world forget, or did it simply not care? As I thought about these questions, I had no answers and no consolation. I even began to ask myself, where is God amidst this dark and evil night?

"How could this happen in a Christian nation?" I wondered. Three years earlier, Pope John Paul II had visited Rwanda. We felt blessed then; the good people of Rwanda had been chosen to greet the pastor of the universal church. No one knew then that His Holiness's message of peace had fallen on infertile soil. I was angry at those who called themselves "Christians" but actively participated in the slaughter. While the religious leaders were not the chief organizers of the genocide, they failed to act in the face of evil. I was angry for their silence, for their passive behavior.

The most excruciating feeling was perhaps the mixture of anger and guilt I felt at the thought of the children I loved but failed to shield from death. My siblings Rose and Regis were the babies of my family. For many years before Regis was born, Rose was the youngest sibling out of six children; for that reason, she was to some extent spoiled and always protected. Like most children at the end of the sibling spectrum, she was charming, affectionate, naïve and very innocent. Her naïve character was, however, fully compensated by her radiant personality and her social skills. The last words she was heard saying very innocently before her death still resonated in my ears: "Why are they doing this? What have we done?" My soul ached at the thought of the suffering she and Regis endured.

I was fourteen and already gone to boarding school when Regis was born. I remember the letter my father sent me informing me of the good news, but since I would go home only for school breaks, I missed seeing my little brother growing up. He was eight when I finished college and started my busy professional life. I did not get to show him things I longed to see when I was his age, like going to the stadium for a soccer game, or watching the lights of the city at night, or riding an elevator. Occasionally when I visited my parents in the South, I would bring him back with me to my house in Kigali. The weekend preceding the Rwandan president's plane crash was one of these moments. Christine and I were driving from the city of Butare; we stopped by my parents' house and took Regis with us to visit my sister Chantal in Kigali. Rose was already at Chantal's house, helping with their baby. We did not know then that we were seeing these children for the last time.

Christine's siblings were no stranger to fear and persecution, given the history of their native Bugesera region, yet they were happy and full of hope. Two months before the start of the genocide, they were forced to flee their home in the southeast, and some of them found refuge at my house in Kigali. For the short period of time we were together, I had the best company I have ever had. We played games, they told me stories, and we laughed. They were full of life, full of love. They became my own brothers and sisters. But eventually they had to go back home when calm returned to their region. When the genocide started in the spring, I prayed for them, pleading for their safety, but the unbelievable had happened: Six of them were killed. Six beautiful, loving, innocent children, the youngest being just six years old.

A light in my soul went dark. My little brothers and sisters perished for no reason. These children had a long and promising life ahead of them. But they were gone forever. There would be no graduation party for them, no excitement for their first job or promotion, no wedding, and no children. No more reason to celebrate their successes and achievements.

During the whole span of these tragic times I never lost my Catholic faith, but I must confess that for some time after the genocide, I found it hard to pray and often lived my life without reference to God. I did not reach the point of rejecting God. I simply did not feel spiritually available to live the faith I inherited from birth and that I learned and practiced throughout my life. Faith was on hold. It was not a deliberate decision. It was just the way it was. I felt as if I were hanging in a giant void. Total emptiness surrounded me. Now the painful reality was settling in, and I realized these killers had truly accomplished their macabre objective: annihilation. They had stripped us of one of the most wonderful gifts God has ever given us: joy. To answer Christine's question: No, life did not actually have any meaning anymore.

PART III

Resurrection

Our wedding day on January 1, 1995.

23

Life Must Go On

Several months had passed, and the country was coming back to life. Time was flying by; and before we knew it, the year was inching toward its end. Some people, mostly foreigners, started telling survivors to move on, to forget the past. They feared that remembering the past would destroy survivors' lives and make reconciliation impossible.

But most of the survivors I met believed that forgetting or ignoring the past was not the answer; they wanted to be heard and understood. They had a strong desire to live with the memory of their loved ones, to honor their lives and restore their dignity. The need to tell their stories was obvious. It was a healing process.

I felt the same way. Memory helped us assume control over the circumstances. There was never a single minute after the genocide I did not think of the loved ones we lost. Though it was painful, I could not ignore their memories; such recollections not only kept them alive for me, but they kept me alive. Now I couldn't live without these memories; they represented my new life. A tape of my life with my family and friends now gone kept playing in my mind.

Going back to work had helped us cope with our grief. After the new government was sworn in, I was promoted to chief of staff within the commerce department. Christine found a new job at the National Insurance Company. The new administration had a huge task to tackle: rebuilding everything. There was a shortage of workers, because many had been killed, and many more had fled the country. Most of the workers were new and inexperienced. Consequently we were busy. It felt surreal to transition from death to normal work, to mix the normal with the abnormal, but we had to make it work. We found that the mind has extraordinary abilities.

During evenings and weekends, Christine and I would spend hours reliving the past. It became a regular routine through which I learned every detail about each of her deceased family members. She did the same about mine. All our conversations were about those we lost; we never tired of discussing our recent history, although tragic; on the contrary, the remembrance energized our spirits.

We would go back to Nyanza to put flowers on my mother's grave and pray. It was a moment of peace and serenity. I felt now that both my mother and Christine's mother were together, watching over us. Their bodies might still be buried in the ground here on earth, but their spirits were already in heaven. They were sending us a message: That our lives still had a meaning. They reminded us of why we survived and that we had responsibilities—responsibilities for building a new life and creating a synergy for happiness, within our family and in the community.

I couldn't reconcile my mother's wonderful spirit with the possibility of permanent death. Something deep inside me refused to admit this was the end. In my mind, I made the tactical decision not to think of our loved ones as gone forever. They were not lost, and they would never die. They would always look like the last time I saw them. Eternally present.

Perhaps at that moment I understood in a personal and profound way what my faith proclaims, that our bodies are transitory and our spirits enduring. That warm realization brought me hope and peace. It engraved in my mind the notion that nothing is ever lost, that the purpose of this transitional life is to prepare us for happy existence after death.

The idea that there is a resurrection had always uplifted me. It's a sacred belief I was taught ever since I was a child and lived with my entire life. But I had found myself recently putting all references to God and his mysteries in the background. I remembered all the prayers I had said while sitting on the ground behind my house, awaiting execution by presidential guards. I thought of the prayers I had said at the Swiss Village and the Mille Collines Hotel when we were surrounded by mobs of ruthless killers. Now was not the time to drift away. I had to be grateful for being alive, for having Christine beside me and a whole future before us. I decided to renew my faith. I was not to live a hopeless, pointless existence. I owed it to the parents who raised me and taught me to obey and love God. I owed it to Christine, who never failed to believe despite the tragic experience she suffered; and I owed it to the beautiful children I knew God was to give us.

Gradually, Christine and I regained strength. People we met, particularly foreigners, asked us many questions. "How can you still function and live your life after what happened? How can you endure the pain?" I did not know what to answer. I was not sure if I had any capacity to conquer pain. What I knew was that renewing my faith and believing in a happy future had allowed me to view grief as temporary and to manage the pain that emanates from it, to the point where it would not overwhelm me.

The painful stories were still there, vivid and bare; but they had gradually become gentle and harmless memories, safely stored in drawers I had somehow created in my mind. Over time, I had acquired the capacity to compartmentalize in my head the sources of my sorrow, while keeping active the sources of my hope.

Now it was the end of 1994 and the most dolorous phases of shock, denial, and anger of the earlier months seemed over. My permanent state of sorrow had gradually evaporated like the morning dew. Initially I felt guilty for letting it go and allowing for normalcy. But I came to realize that this was not my choice. The frozen bubble in my mind had started to melt and I was gradually adjusting to reality. Acceptance was settling in, and life was to go on.

Somehow, I felt liberated. I was no longer stuck with tragedy and with that realization came an unshakable peace. It was as though I had been given the keys to hope. It was a feeling of renewal, of life.

Christine and I felt the time had come to fulfill the commitment we made to our families and to God. We had a renewed sense of purpose, strengthened by the realization that we had the power to sustain life through love.

On January 1, 1995, we were married. Christine had picked the day: "A new year, a new beginning," as she rightly put it. On that sunny first Sunday of the new year, we walked side by side into the St. Michel Cathedral in Kigali to the sound of a beautiful song by the Kigali chorus. The church was filled mostly with relatives who had recently returned from exile, and with acquaintances and even strangers. The list of our invitees was short, but we were pleasantly surprised by the large number of attendees. Many of our fellow survivors of the Mille Collines Hotel were present. Most had heard about the wedding and showed up just to express their solidarity and support.

People stood and sang with the chorus as we slowly walked down the aisle. We all had on our minds the double meaning of the moment: a triumph of life over death and a tribute to loving family members, lost too soon. Christine squeezed hard on my hand and I sensed she was overcome by emotions. I tightly held her hand while fighting back my own tears. Once again, the devastation of the genocide was very much felt. Of all the people who had attended our engagement ceremony a year ago, only a handful survived to attend the wedding. It was a vivid reminder of the depth of the tragedy.

I had prepared myself mentally for this moment. Now was not the time to think of death and desolation. I forcefully chose to push away sentiments of grief and to embrace the new chapter I was about to enter with my wife-to-be. No, the loved ones we lost were not dead. Right now they were watching over us. I felt their invisible presence, loving and supportive.

A few months back I did not know whether I would live to see this day. Throughout the wedding ceremony, which was officiated by my uncle, Father Hermenegilde, I silently said prayers of gratitude. I was grateful for the life I had been given and for having my beautiful bride next to me. I thanked God for giving me his most precious gift: the ability to love. When the time came to say "I do," I said it with a special meaning, absolutely certain about my love for my wife and the sacrifices I was ready to make for her well-being. I genuinely asked God to guide us and allow us to see the beauty and good in the life before us. At the same occasion, we celebrated the baptism of my nephew, Steve; Christine and I were his sponsors.

The reception was held at the Diplomat Hotel, the same place I had gone to on April 14, desperately looking for help. I was running for my life then, chased by mad, armed men looking for money or my skin. It was then a dangerous lions' den, where the genocidal government and the army had moved their central command. It had been a terrifying place and a desperate moment, as I did not even know if my fiancée was still alive; but now it was a taste of heaven. I was surrounded by friendly and loving faces, and, most importantly, I had my bride beside me. The same setting that had instilled fear in the recent past was now a place of celebration, filled with hope and the promise of renewed life.

Christine and I did not have a honeymoon. It was not a time for such a luxury. This was not the wedding we had dreamed of, but in many perspectives, we were grateful, for being alive and for being together. The wedding was our bridge back to life. It was

January 1, 1995. Christine and I are married. "A new year, a new beginning," she said.

the beginning of a chapter that we wanted to a resurrection for us as well as for others. Several of our surviving relatives, mostly younger siblings and cousins, were staying with us in our home. We did not have much, and our meager paychecks only covered a small portion of our needs.

The responsibility to care for the large household was overwhelming, but so were the needs of survivors. Despite the enormity of the task, we were willing to expand our reach and share what we had. Our siblings and cousins brought other young people almost every day. In them I could see hope for the future; I could see life.

In every town and throughout the countryside, however, many children lived alone or under the supervision of their minor relatives in difficult conditions. Christine's sister Clementine and her friend Jeanne, now back in their native Bugesera, would describe the situation of the children as alarming. Most of these children had had a normal upbringing; nothing could have prepared them for the tough life they were living now.

Among these children were cousins of Jeanne. The youngest, Carine, was just eight years old. She lost both her parents, who were teachers at the local elementary school. She was among the few who survived the killings in the Bugesera swamp. Every time they brought her for a visit, she lit up our house; she was a real source of joy.

Eventually some children ended up living with older relatives. We learned Carine was taken in by a cousin, Delphine, a woman widowed by the genocide. But like many, she had limited means and children of her own to take care of. To complicate matters, she lived near a swamp at the edge of the capital, an area infested by malaria-bearing mosquitoes, the number one killer in the country. Not surprisingly, Carine started getting sick. We briefly had her at our home, and she got better. But whenever she returned, she got sick again.

One day Delphine told us that Carine's condition was complicated and she was admitted at the King Faisal Hospital, one of the few functioning medical facilities in the country. But the hospital was running at its full capacity. It was the only health facility that could house the hundreds of patients in need of treatment for different types of illness. Unfortunately, after the genocide, there were not enough doctors and nurses to treat everybody. The beds and mattresses had been looted, and the hospital was short on medication. If anybody got out of the hospital alive, it was more by miracle than by the care received.

Christine and I entered one of the rooms and saw Carine lying on a thin blanket on the hard floor. She had been hooked up to an IV; fluids in a plastic bag were flowing through a tube right into her tiny arm. Now she looked no more than five, and really sick. She had chills and was sweating; she complained of headache and looked exhausted and very weak. She had a continuous fever and was having slight convulsions. We immediately knew she had malaria. Delphine had already left the hospital because she had other children to watch at home; she had left Carine with a mother who was attending to her sick child in the same room. Before we left, we asked a nurse passing by to keep an eye on the child.

On our way out of the hospital, Christine looked at me but said nothing. But I knew what she was thinking. We walked in silence to the parking lot and sat in the car for a few minutes, allowing ourselves a moment of reflection before hitting the streets. When Christine said what was on her mind, I agreed without hesitation. We were going to take Carine home and make sure she got all the attention she needed. We took it as a responsibility, a commitment to a father and a mother we never knew, who gave it all to educate Rwandan children but were not given the chance to raise their own little girl. It was a commitment to a God we had constantly asked for protection while in distress, and made promises to submit to his will if we survived. Delphine gladly accepted our proposal. We did not have enough resources and were trying to start our life over, but we were hopeful for a better future. Days later, Carine joined our home. Christine's friend Claire, a nurse at the insurance company where they both worked, volunteered to come to our house and give Carine two shots every day. Within a week she was better. We enrolled her in a good school not far from our home. She was a joyful little girl with a contagious laugh.

Very soon we learned from Clemence about a young boy also

orphaned by the genocide who lived on a military base in the South. He had relatives, but none of them was ready or had the means to support him. Clemence did not need a lot of convincing to get the boy into our house. So Claude, a quiet eleven-year-old boy, joined us in early 1995. We put him in school as well. By the end of that month, we had a few more relatives in our house. We did not mind.

Our household grew in numbers and in strength. It was filled every day with sounds of life, of revival. It was a remarkable rebirth, much of which I attributed to Christine. She was only a young newlywed, but she had become like a mother to our surviving siblings, cousins, and all these orphans now under our roof. It was a difficult role for someone working full time. But she was a blessing for everyone around her. I saw in her the portrait of both of our mothers, two women of grace and humility who exhibited a wonderful spirit of kindness and compassion. I had no doubt the two mothers were watching over her, guiding her in every move. I was comforted with the thought that they were up there, passionately pleading for my family with a God they had loved and trusted their entire lives, who would always lend them a sympathetic ear. We were blessed, and I couldn't ask for more.

But we were granted more. On a beautiful day that spring of 1995, Christine told me that she was pregnant. The revelation filled my soul with intense joy. It was a feeling I had never experienced before. The notion that Christine and I were the bearers of life after the experience of total extinction was overpowering. God was entrusting us with the gift of sustaining life and enjoying it in a profound way. I was ready to accept it fully. It was a humbling and exciting new beginning.

24

Live and Let Live

It was now nearly one year after the start of the genocide, and I had regained confidence in the possibility of living a happy and productive life. My confidence was enhanced by the exciting thought of soon becoming a parent. All around us I could see signs of life bursting forth. It was tempting to jump in the course of the blossoming life and follow a self-centered path, but no one with any conscience could ignore the call to address the injury that had befallen so many innocent people. In my view, every able man and woman had an obligation to lend a hand.

As I reflected on the gift of life I was given, I knew I needed to get involved in a cause reaching far beyond the well-being of my household. Already around the country, brave men and women were at work, making a difference in a broken world that needed fixing.

Among them were Christine's aunt, Sister Teya, and Father Jerome Masinzo, a Catholic priest in the Butare diocese. In the aftermath of the genocide, they became a great source of inspiration for me. Teya had lived a long life of compassion and love for the poor. She joined the Little Sisters of Jesus in the 1960s when she was only seventeen. Since then, she had dedicated her life to the well-being of the most vulnerable members of society. She spent several years in dense forests of central Africa, living with marginalized groups, such as pygmies. She learned a lot about the fundamental values of life. She traveled the world extensively, learning and teaching the Bible. In Rwanda, she initiated projects to spiritually rehabilitate street boys and give household workers the dignity they deserved. With her, I discovered true humility and a renewed sense of service.

In the aftermath of the genocide, Teya noted that many people were occupied only with self-preservation, with no consideration whatsoever of the dignity and generosity that once characterized the people of Rwanda. Mistrust among people had risen, and any sense of humanity was being lost.

Teya was very much concerned with the social trajectory people in the community were embarking on. Our common cohesion was falling apart, and the center couldn't hold anymore. Something needed to be done, and she thought the survivors should play a central role in repositioning that trajectory on the right track.

"After the genocide, I felt like the way I did things before could no longer give satisfaction," Teya told me at one of the many visits Christine and I paid her.

"I think our way of living, of thinking, of getting involved in society, should never be the same again. If I was not killed, it's because the Lord has a project for me. This project is for me to offer my life to others."

The turning point for Teya came when she learned of the work Father Jerome was doing for a rural community of traumatized Tutsi widows in the Karama commune, south of Butare. Jerome had started an association for these women, which he called *Courage de vivre* ("Courage to live"), with the purpose of giving these women, who had lost their husbands and children at the hands of their Hutu neighbors, a forum to meet and regain strength.

Jerome's own story of survival was captivating and inspiring. When the genocide started in 1994, he was pastor of the Ngoma parish in Butare. He gave shelter at his parish to hundreds of Tutsi refugees fleeing massacres and fed them for a couple of weeks. On April 30, the parish was attacked by mobs armed with all sorts of weapons. They killed almost all the refugees, including men, women, and children. Jerome climbed in the ceiling of his house at the parish and hid there for several days. Jerome was a tall and large man. One night, the ceiling collapsed under his heavy weight, and he fell on top of the pots and pans in the kitchen, making a tremendous clatter, and injuring himself in the process. The parish cook and a second priest at the parish took care of him and hid him in a drawer mounted in a wall in the church. The killers looked for him everywhere but did not find him.

After the genocide, Jerome restarted his pastoral ministry at the Ngoma parish. Later, he went to a neighboring parish, whose pastor had been assassinated, to help the faithful. When he got there, he found desolation. There was still blood on the walls of the church. He could see human flesh and hair on the walls. Survivors were traumatized and desperate. Most were children and women who had lost their husbands and almost all their relatives. Their houses had been destroyed, and they were left with nothing. These widows had become aggressive; they would throw stones at the wives of the men, now in prison, responsible for the massacres.

This was a Catholic community, but almost none of the survivors wanted to enter the church. Their conscience had rebelled; God was on the dock. Where was he in their miseries? All they saw was evil. "Evil has won in this country; evil has planted its flag on each hill," they would say. Instead of starting to celebrate Mass as usual, Jerome thought he needed to talk to the widows. He invited them one by one and listened to their stories. Many had been raped; they still had fresh wounds from machetes; their children had been mutilated. Their stories were horrifying; it was the procession to Calvary. They cried as they told their stories. But Jerome encouraged them to talk, and he cried with them. He later brought them together as a group and encouraged them to listen to one another and find positive, inspirational moments in their stories. He provided his own example of survival, talking about amazing people who helped him survive.

Jerome, who knew Teya as a Bible scholar, invited her to come and teach these women the Bible. Teya did not hesitate. She devoted her time listening to the women, reliving their stories, and understanding their anger and sorrow. She prayed with them, read them the Bible, and taught them how to put their dolorous experiences in the context of the scriptures.

"At first, they were skeptical," Teya told me. "Their resignation to fate and their anger toward Hutu women whose husbands were in prison, accused of involvement in the killings, were consuming them. But I began to progress after we started reading the Bible and sharing our stories. They realized I had lived the same experiences and seen the same horrors. I, too, had family members; this helped solidify trust between us. Gradually they listened and actively participated in our talks. I began to see in them a renewed sense of belief in their ability to live fully again."

Teya explained that the next step was to work on forgiveness and reconciliation. She knew it was not going to be easy. The divide was still deep; some of the Hutu women were suspected of having blood on their hands. Many had willingly supported their husbands in committing horrible crimes; others had betrayed to the killers the Tutsi families hiding in their homes. "*Nyagasani azabidushoboza*" ("the Lord will help us make it happen"), Teya added, with conviction and a warm smile.

Teya and Jerome's inspiring story opened my eyes. People were hurting, and it did not take much to alleviate their suffering. With just a Bible, a little time, and maybe a smile, Teya and Jerome were rebuilding lives. Wasn't that the kind of work we should be doing? I wanted to get involved. Teya and Jerome knew exactly what else that community needed: roofs over their heads.

Weeks later Teya introduced me to Jerome. He was a tall and large man, yet with a palpable sense of humility. His kind face was a reflection of his beautiful soul. They invited me to visit the *Courage de vivre* association. They said they had been thinking about building houses for the widows and thought I could be of some help. I immediately agreed to get involved, confident I could use some of my contacts in the capital to help this great cause.

We drove to the Karama commune on a long and dusty road through steep hills and deep valleys. As soon as we reached the top of a chain of hills, I knew we had arrived. Not a single house was still standing. The scarce bananas trees were skinny and fruitless; the hills were bushy, and weeds had taken over the abandoned fields. There were no cows, no goats or sheep. No birds either. Life seemed to have evaporated from this cropless land.

The widows came from nowhere and greeted us with broken smiles and tight hugs. Soon I saw where they lived. Teya explained that this place used to be a pigsty. The conditions were beyond deplorable. For a moment, I forgot about any challenges I had ever faced; all my problems became relatively small.

Back in Kigali I spoke with a representative of the Red Cross I had met at a government meeting. It did not take any convincing to get his attention. The Red Cross was already involved in reconstruction projects in the country; he agreed to provide construction material and transportation. Back in Butare, Teya and Jerome were making their own contacts and organizing the widows, explaining what role they should play in the reconstruction.

We picked a site in Karama and symbolically dug the first foundation. The real work would start the next day. The women started making mud bricks and cutting wood. In the weeks that followed, the Red Cross delivered on its promise, providing the first construction material. I couldn't wait to see the project come to fruition.

Father Jerome and Sister Teya.

25

Remember—Do Not Hold Grudges

My sense of responsibility and moral commitment grew from the Karama experience. I developed a strong desire to make survivors' issues my own and to be part of the solution. The most pressing issues were related to physical and psychological wounds. It was hard to watch children, teenagers, and women with deep machete cuts or struggling with trauma. I wanted to join forces with others to help rehabilitate the most vulnerable among the survivors and get them support in their struggle to live again.

There was already a platform we could use to get started. The period before the genocide had seen the rise of human rights associations, one of which was Kanyarwanda, a well-known organization whose goal was to promote unity through social justice. I had joined Kanyarwanda shortly after it was established in 1991, inspired by Ignace Ruhatana and Fidele Kanyabugoyi, two great men I respected for their moral values and bravery. They were nationally recognized for standing for human rights in dangerous times of political turmoil. Unfortunately, Ruhatana, a moderate Hutu, and Kanyabugoyi, a Tutsi, were both killed during the genocide; so were several other members of the association. Now, more than ever, the important work they had started had to continue. We owed these pioneers of social justice a continuous commitment toward a more just society.

I went on a quest to find any surviving members of Kanyarwanda. I found a few. To them we added new members and revived the association and its board, which I was chosen to chair. We worked as volunteers, with no pay, but we were highly motivated by the opportunity to help others. Because of the needs of the moment, our priority became helping wounded survivors get medical treatment and counseling.

We launched a medical care project, whose work consisted of finding modest financial support for people with severe injuries and connecting them with medical facilities in the country or abroad. The work was rewarding but overwhelming; we needed a full-time coordinator. I thought of someone who I knew could be a fantastic fit: Sister Cecile Nyiragasani, a nun of the Little Sisters of Jesus, whom I had met while visiting Sister Teya. When I approached her she did not hesitate to take on the challenge. But not everyone cheered her involvement. Sister Cecile was a Hutu, and some people familiar with our work took issue with the notion that she could possibly love and care for Tutsi survivors. My friends at Kanyarwanda and I were shocked by this attitude from the very same people who experienced and suffered from ethnic discrimination. "Sister Cecile is a hero among us," we would tell them. "We should all be thankful for her generosity and big heart." Sister Cecile truly embodied the new society Rwanda could become; a society driven by love and a sense of humanity.

Sister Cecile ended up doing a wonderful job. She would take pictures of the victims and their wounds, write up their story, and send it to organizations willing to help. Thanks to her efforts, hundreds of survivors, many of them bearing terrible wounds, or with bullets lodged inside their bodies, received medical care.

Similar initiatives were launched by individuals and local associations, and great progress was made. But the amount of work to be done was as vast as the ocean. Gradually it became obvious a more vigorous response was needed. Other survivors working and living in the capital shared the same concern and the same passion to keep telling the story of the genocide. We would meet after work at my office and brainstorm about our role as survivors and what contribution we could bring. We hoped to persuade decision makers at the national and international levels to allocate resources to help survivors find healing, whether physical or psychological. It was the right thing to do, and it could facilitate the reconciliation process we knew was important and that the international community was urging Rwanda to embrace.

Among the most vocal entities pushing for urgent reconciliation was the United Nations, the very same organization that had failed Rwanda, refusing to act when the genocide was under way and abandoning people in danger when they most needed protection. Now perhaps the UN could redeem itself by helping survivors. When the secretary general of the United Nations, Boutros Boutros-Ghali, visited Rwanda in 1995, our group of survivors asked permission to meet him. We wanted to convey our feelings to one of the most powerful dealers in the world.

The honor of meeting the secretary general fell on me and François Nduwumwe, a friend and fellow survivor at the Mille Collines Hotel. We met Boutros-Ghali at the Kigali airport before he boarded his plane back to New York. We told him many survivors were hurting, that there were tears and suffering; we wanted to hear from him what the UN intended to do to help alleviate the physical and psychological damage left by a tragedy the international community could have prevented. The secretary general was quickly on the defensive. He indicated that his organization did not owe anything to Rwanda, that the people of Rwanda owned their destiny. He indulged himself in a vague monologue that left us wondering if he was detached from reality or if he had chosen to adopt an attitude of calculated ambiguity. He did not offer any word of sympathy or support. We were dismayed by his lack of empathy and his detachment from the suffering caused by a tragedy that happened under his watch. As Rwandans, we understood we had our destiny in our hands, but at the same time we hoped the international community would go the extra mile to pull us back from the abyss we were thrown into by the genocide. In our opinion, that was a realistic expectation.

It was clear that the much-needed help would not come from abroad. It did not seem that the world even understood or was willing to hear what really happened during the genocide and how much the country and the survivors were hurting. Rwanda was a small player among all nations; its problems were of little consequence on the world stage. That was the sad reality. Perhaps also the genocide was an embarrassing topic for the international community that had to be pushed under the rug.

But we would not sit idle and wait for the world to suddenly change and to come to our rescue. It was up to us, Rwandans and survivors in particular, to roll up our sleeves and find solutions to the various problems we were facing. We needed to strengthen our capabilities by creating a dynamic civil society. There had been so far a few initiatives by some survivors to tackle challenges specific to their own groups. Widows had just formed an association, called AVEGA, to help its members and their children on various issues. Survivors living in Belgium had created IBUKA-Belgique, an association that was to focus on justice and memory. It was obvious, however, that we needed a solid organization that could coordinate the response to all important issues caused by the genocide and gather adequate support. Survivors' needs were endless. Their physical and psychological wounds were deep; they had lost their homes and all other possessions; orphans had to be taken care of and get an education; but, most importantly, survivors needed hope and a renewed sense of purpose. Our goal was to put in place such an organization to represent the survivors as well as the victims. To the survivors, we owed support and solidarity. To the dead we owed remembrance, respect, and the perpetuation of their legacy.

I initiated formal meetings with a larger group of survivors working in Kigali, many of whom I had recently worked with to help organize the very first commemoration of the genocide in Kigali. We all had the same vision. We understood our lives now called for responsibilities we never thought would rest on our shoulders. Fulfilling these responsibilities required a sense of selflessness and service to others. We met and brainstormed every day after work and on weekends, reflecting on our vision for the future and on the need to remember the past so as to avoid its repetition. The future we envisioned was based on healing the past, instead of burying it, creating a space to start anew and promote a just and tolerant society.

After several months of work, we had drafted in detail the vision we proposed to follow, the concrete actions we planned to take, and the legal framework of the organization we wanted to put in place to carry out our mission.

At that time Christine was in her last month of pregnancy. On the morning of November 29, 1995, she gave birth to our daughter Christelle Fiona. For the first time after the genocide, I was overwhelmed by joy. As I took my baby in my arms and held her against my chest, I couldn't contain my emotions. So recently I had doubted that Christine and I would live to see this day. But once again the God of creation had blessed us with the precious gift of life. The arrival of that child promised to erase the pain of the past and create new memories. It was the beginning of a whole new future.

Becoming a parent renewed for me the sense of purpose. I was no longer a victim. I felt energized and ready to take on the challenges of helping others rebuild their lives. It was with optimism and energy that I proceeded to carry out the mission of working with my fellow survivors toward putting in place the organization we envisioned. To the various associations of survivors and to other people of goodwill, we made an appeal to join in this initiative.

Speaking at a conference of the UN Industrial Development Organization (UNIDO) in Vienna, Austria; a plea to help Rwanda heal and develop economically was at the center of my message.

On a beautiful day in December of 1995, a large crowd of men and women from diverse backgrounds, mostly survivors, responded to our call and gathered in Kigali and pledged to work toward a world of peace, to promote justice and fairness, to support the most vulnerable among survivors, and to preserve the memory and the noble legacy of the victims. Those who answered our call were civil servants, healthcare professionals, teachers, lawyers, members of the clergy, businessmen, and ordinary citizens. We called our organization IBUKA ("Remember"). It was to serve as the umbrella organization grouping all survivors' associations and individuals willing to fight genocide ideology, to stand for justice, to be the guardian and support for orphans and widows, and to give hope and a sense of belonging.

I was satisfied with the outcome and considered my work done. I did not intend to lead the organization. I had helped put it in place and I wanted others take the lead in implementing the vision we had just articulated. I had promised Christine I would now be more available to be at her side. But no one among my peers volunteered to lead the organization. When the gathering overwhelmingly asked me to play that role, I accepted and was elected chair of the organization for a three-year period. I would have to explain and apologize to Christine. She was supportive.

We did not waste any time. With other members of IBUKA's board, we made a commitment to visit survivors in all corners of the country, to listen to their stories, to learn their needs, and help them regain the hope and confidence they needed to get back up on their feet.

For several months, we set out to find survivors wherever they lived, in various towns around the country, in small commercial centers, or deep in the hills of the countryside. They were happy to meet fellow survivors. The deep scars on their bodies showed the physical pain they endured. Their psychological wounds were invisible but palpable. Some were ashamed of their wounds and of the humiliation they had suffered, as if it were their fault.

For many of these survivors, life as they knew it did not exist anymore. Many families were quasi extinct; properties had been destroyed; almost nothing that connected to the past could be found—no pictures of the victims, no personal belongings. Every trace of life had been erased. These survivors were crushed under the weight of loss, grief, and humiliation. They seemed lost, disoriented, and defeated by pain and sorrow. Most appeared resigned to their fate and had lost faith in humanity and in their ability to rebuild their lives.

Revenge was never on their mind. They wanted justice. They did not ask for any material things. They just wanted to tell their stories and lay their loved ones to rest.

I found that the best gift you can offer a survivor is to listen to his or her story. We took the time. Almost every story started with the moment the country learned of the death of the president on the morning of April 7, 1994. From there everyone would tell a personal narrative of what happened next, often in a detailed and passionate way. For some survivors, the stories were too painful to tell; the recollection of what they went through was a burden too heavy to bear. Nevertheless, they wanted their stories told. We listened intently, not missing a word. The stories described the fear that preceded the attacks by the army or the Interahamwe militia, the brutality of the assaults, the chaos, the separation from family members, the hiding, the rejection by neighbors unwilling to help, the wandering in the open space, the prayers, and eventually the rescue by the RPF or by other good people, ready to help, despite the danger.

I listened to stories of women who lost their husbands and their children, of men who lost their limbs fighting to protect their loved ones, of young survivors who lost their parents. I listened to widows who never lost faith in God, and I was inspired by their spirit of love and forgiveness. In spite of their loss and struggles, they always kept a dignified demeanor. I admired the bravery of these men who put their lives on the line to protect others.

We helped survivors grieve and lay to rest their loved ones. With the help of the government, bodies were disinterred from mass graves and buried in dignity in memorial sites. We wanted the victims to be remembered and respected and their life stories shared; and we wanted to know how many souls were lost. We started surveys in some regions that had large Tutsi populations and put together a list of victims by family. The aim was to extend the work to the rest of the country, no matter how many years it would take.

We knew survivors needed more than emotional support. We had no means to directly help survivors, but we had a voice and a compelling story to tell, and we knew we could count on the support of several political leaders. Many were survivors themselves or had helped defeat the previous genocidal regime. The most effective way to address survivors' issues, we thought, was to have a national fund to which Rwandans, including survivors, businesses operating in Rwanda, the Rwandan government, and the international community would contribute. Additionally, we believed survivors in general, regardless of their social status, deserved to receive reparations. We pushed these ideas during the 1995 conference held in Kigali on "Genocide: Dialogue for a National and International Response," the first of its kind to genuinely search for a viable and coherent solution to the problems faced by Rwanda in the aftermath of the genocide. While the conference did not adopt any resolution on reparations, it recommended the creation of a national fund to assist needy individuals within the survivors' community. As a result, the government of Rwanda established the *Fonds d'assistance aux rescapés du génocide—FARG*. The fund's objective was to help the most vulnerable among survivors, Tutsi and moderate Hutu alike, from rebuilding their houses to providing medical assistance and supporting children's education.

IBUKA was to play a central role in administering the fund. The minister in charge of family promotion, Aloysia Inyumba, asked me soon after the adoption of the law establishing FARG to provide the names of three of the five administrators of the fund. I was happy to nominate people of the highest integrity among IBUKA members: Esther Mujawayo, a widow of the genocide, Antoine Mugesera, survivor and politician, and Anglican bishop Alexis Bilindabagabo.

The establishment of the fund was one of the most important decisions ever made in the postgenocide era that was to impact the lives of survivors. Tens of thousands of young survivors were able to complete high school, thousands attended college, and thousands of houses were rebuilt. The assistance, however, was only a drop in the ocean, considering all the problems survivors faced.

Meanwhile, the international community, perhaps still feeling ashamed for not stepping in to stop the genocide, continued to drag its feet. When President Bill Clinton came to Rwanda on March 26, 1998, he gave a moving speech in which he acknowledged that "the international community, together with nations in Africa, must bear its share of responsibility for this tragedy." I was there at the Kigali airport, among the couple of hundred diplomats and Rwandan officials invited to listen to the speech. I remember being moved to tears, as the U.S. president spoke directly to survivors, acknowledged the mistakes made, and promised to act to remedy the consequences of genocide: "We cannot change the past. But we can and must do everything in our power to help you build a future without fear, and full of hope," he said. He pledged to support the genocide survivors' fund and urged other nations to do the same, so that "survivors and their communities can find the care they need and the help they must have." I was hopeful after Mr. Clinton's visit. But as time went by, survivors lowered their expectations as no material support came from the international community to specifically improve their lives.

We were not to be deterred by the lack of sufficient external support. We urged all people of goodwill to continue to lend us a hand and give more survivors, particularly children, a chance to improve their lives. Many families stepped in and raised orphans and surrounded them with love and care. Many wounded survivors received care in Rwanda or abroad, with the support of small contributions. IBUKA and its member associations organized and trained volunteers around the country to rebuild houses, provide psychological counseling, offer legal support, put children in school, and serve as ambassadors of hope. Gradually we helped many survivors connect and recover from grief, anger, and guilt. They developed a sense of belonging and started regaining confidence.

On one of my trips to the South, I reconnected with Sister Teya and Father Jerome about the construction project we had initiated in the Karama commune. I was amazed to witness the transformation that had occurred. Nearly two hundred houses had been built, with a very significant contribution from the widows themselves. Most importantly, thanks to the Bible study and dialogue about reconciliation they had with Sister Teya, these women had recovered from the anger and resentment they had toward the wives of the men responsible for the killings. The story of the widows of Karama became one of the positive stories of the postgenocide era. We celebrated the rebirth of that community joyfully and with fanfare. The prime minister and the bishop of Butare got word of the project and insisted on being there on inauguration day and pledged their support. Since then, life blossomed. When Teya, Jerome, and I returned several weeks later, we were greeted by the sounds of life: people laughing, children playing, cows mooing, and roosters crowing.

Around the country, similar projects were under way, supported by local communities, political leaders, or the church. Putting everything into perspective, there was cause to be grateful. The genocide fell upon us unexpectedly; the country and its citizens were certainly not equipped to tackle most of the issues, and no one among us was prepared to inherit the grave consequences of one of the greatest tragedies in human history. Yet, we had come together to rebuild our lives. With very few resources we had restored smiles on people's faces. We had discovered within us the humanity we did not know we had. We all felt good in our hearts.

Every evening we went to our families and looked into the eyes of our spouses and children, proud of the work we had done. I was grateful to Christine for her understanding and patience. The love and support she showed me kept me going. She had now given birth to our second daughter, Chelsea. I was forever grateful for the gift of life I was given and the blessings of sustaining life our God showered on us. Once I wondered if life had a meaning. Now I had the answer.

Top: Summer 1998. With Christine and our children, Fiona (two and a half years old) and Chelsea (one year old).

Bottom: Becoming U.S. citizens. Left to right: our daughters Fiona, Chelsea, Carine, Tracy (front), Christine and I.

Epilogue

A New Life in a New World

Iimmigrated to the United States with my family in the fall of 2000 and settled in New Hampshire, where my sister Chantal and her six-year-old son Steve had preceded us two years earlier. We were welcomed by a spectacular show of the New England fall foliage. In contrast with my image of a highly urbanized landscape, I was pleasantly surprised to see this side of America. The wooded landscape offered a sense of serenity and peace.

I was struck by how friendly they people were toward my family and how genuinely they wished us well. Most declared that they themselves came from families of immigrants, and I quickly felt a sense of belonging. I was surprised to learn that many were people of faith. The notion I had vaguely heard that Americans had drifted away from God was definitely untrue. That realization comforted me and convinced me even more that I had brought my family to the right place.

We enrolled Fiona and Chelsea in school, and soon English started replacing their French. I was eager to be a part of the American family and embrace its best ideals of freedom and cultural diversity. I did not wait long to have a glimpse into a rich experience unique to the American tradition. On a chilly Thursday afternoon in November, friends of my sister Chantal invited my family to our first Thanksgiving in the United States. We sat around the dinner table at their house and shared a sumptuous meal, which consisted of an oven-roasted turkey, mashed potatoes, gravy, green beans, fresh salad, cranberry sauce, and an array of pies and ice cream for dessert. I loved the food, but most importantly, I loved the idea of taking the time to gather in a family setting and acknowledge the good fortune that has been bestowed upon us. I learned that hundreds of millions of people across the nation were gathered the same way, doing the very same thing. The moment was a special one for my family. There was so much to be thankful for. The hell that Christine and I had experienced was behind us now. We had two beautiful little angels next to us, and perhaps more were to come. We were starting a new life built on hope and great aspirations.

I had no illusions about the challenges of starting over in a foreign land, but I was determined to immerse myself and my family in a new way of living, and to give my children a chance of becoming part of a bigger world. Nothing was to deter me from pursuing that goal. Even the freezing weather.

I came to appreciate the beauty of winter, the purity of the air and the serenity of the landscape covered in bright white snow. As I reflected upon it, this was the very essence of life. Storms are part of our lives, and there is nothing we can do to prevent them; but we can learn how to make the best of them; and this is exactly how I was going to approach life in this new and remote country— with an open mind and adjustable attitude.

If I was to survive and raise a family in this new environment, I knew I needed to get a job and earn a regular income. But the very first step was to learn the language. Someone had told me several years ago that English is an easy language that can be learned in just six months. Christine and I would soon find this to be untrue. We took free classes, listened to tapes, watched TV, and most importantly, spoke with people. The listening was not easy. Americans talk fast, as if always in a rush. The speaking was equally challenging. I would translate words from French into English in my mind before formulating a sentence. The learning process was difficult, but it was not an impossible task. Knowing that failure was not an option, Christine and I forced our way through our new language and gradually became more comfortable. We were not ashamed of making errors. I knew I had reached an important milestone when I had my first dream in English! If I was fluent in my sleep, I could well be while awake. It was time to look for employment.

Armed with my college diploma, to which I attached an impressive seven-page curriculum vitae, I approached local companies. I got zero response. Someone told me that hiring managers do not read more than one page. I was taken aback. Who can possibly fit an entire career on a single page? I revised my approach and produced a one-page summary—a resumé, as they call it. But no one was interested in my experiences overseas. The only option now was to go back to school. After a lengthy process of preparing for the necessary entrance exams, I was admitted to the graduate program at the University of New Hampshire's business school. I was grateful for the opportunity and for the timely arrival of a much-needed student loan, which supported my family for a year. By the time I started my second year, I found employment and started a new career while taking part-time classes.

In the summer of 2003 we welcomed our youngest daughter, Tracy. As I held in my arms this new bundle of joy, I thanked God for the blessings he bestowed on Christine and me, giving us the precious gift of becoming parents again.

Our growing family became even larger in the spring of the following year, when we welcomed Carine and Claude, the two children we raised but had to leave behind in Rwanda while awaiting the completion of immigration formalities. We prayed that they would adapt to the new environment, which could be tough on young adults. Carine quickly blended in. In some respects, America was an exact match for her. She had made an effort to learn English, and she transitioned easily into high school and then college. Claude, at twenty-one, was rather challenged to adapt to the expectations and norms of life in a foreign country. He chose to return to Rwanda to live with family members still there.

Gradually our family settled in and immersed themselves into the busy American life, like any other local family. Christine and I were always on the run, between work, evening classes, the grocery store, school open houses, soccer practice, and church. But we enjoyed every moment of it. Our children became our life. We watched them grow and got involved in every aspect of their development, at home, at church, and at school. They loved school and did well. We helped them with homework, just as our parents did for us.

We learned a lot from the process and came to understand and appreciate the story behind the making of America, a story of hardship and courage that forged the character of the American people and unequivocally spread the principles of democracy, freedom, and justice into the world. I wished the people of African nations who led the struggles for independence had fought for the preservation of unity, peace, and human freedom and had not let seeds of hatred invade their land. The recent tragedies did not have to happen. The people of Rwanda did not have to go through genocide.

Our hearts never left Rwanda. All over that land, the story of our life was written in the blood of our loved ones. That story needed to be told: not to lament or to draw sympathy, not to provoke anger or reopen wounds, but to educate and raise awareness about an issue that should concern every decent human being. I felt compelled to be again at the forefront of the campaign against genocide. I spoke at Rotary Clubs, churches, Holocaust memorials, high schools, and universities. Most people were stunned to learn the details of a relatively recent human tragedy to which they had never paid attention. All audiences I spoke to were receptive.

I was encouraged to meet brave men and women committed to end injustice and to promote human rights and dignity. Along with fellow survivors of various genocides and the Holocaust, my family participated in events and rallies aimed at bringing people together to denounce hatred, prejudice, and mass murder. I joined forces with Friends of Rwandan Genocide Survivors—FORGES, a small organization led by three brave Rwandan widows of the genocide—Esperance Uwambyeyi, Christina Mukankaka, and my own sister, Chantal Kayitesi—not only to help young survivors in Rwanda attend school but also to help survivors in our own community, every year in April, to honor the memory of their loved ones and reflect on their legacy through a candle-lighting ceremony. I brought along my children, so they could grow up knowing that no matter what one goes through, you can still surround yourself with love and tolerance.

We cannot undo what was done, but we can strive to prevent it from happening again by planting the seeds of peace and hope. I will always be thankful to God, not only for rescuing Christine and me, and giving us beautiful children, but also for keeping us strong, resilient, and loving. As the great Rev. Dr. Martin Luther King Jr. said, "I have decided to stick with love. Hate is too great a burden to bear."

Remembering the victims of the genocide: Candle-lighting ceremony, Boston, MA. Left to right: my daughter Chelsea, my daughter Tracy, and Christine Mukankata, widow of the genocide and founding member of Friends of Rwandan Genocide Survivors (FORGES).

Laurent Kayijamahe (Christine's uncle) and his family in 1987. L to R: Melanie (Laurent's wife), Rene, Alice (youngest in front), Christine, Josiane, Angelique, Aline, and Laurent. Missing was his second son, Charles. The entire family (except Melanie) was killed during the genocide in 1994.

My sister Rose Mukazi, dressed as a bridesmaid for my sister's wedding. She was killed in April 1994.

Funeral Mass for my mother. Service led by my uncle, Father Hermenegilde, who returned to Rwanda from Burundi after more than thirty years in exile.

Carine went on to attend the University of New Hampshire (UNH) and completed a master's degree in public administration. She met her husband, Marcus Boggis, at UNH and got married in 2013. She has spoken against genocide at various events around New England. The couple gave birth to their little girl, Liana, in 2018.

After graduating from Bishop Guertin High School in Nashua, New Hampshire, Christelle Fiona attended the University of Notre Dame and majored in political science in 2017.

Chelsea graduated from Bishop Guertin High School in Nashua, New Hampshire, and was admitted in the "Behavioral Neuroscience" program at Northeastern University in Boston, Massachusetts, and is aspiring to attend medical school.

My sister Chantal and her son, Steve, immigrated to the United States; Steve graduated from Columbia University in 2016 and is aspiring to attend medical school.

My sister Julienne immigrated to England, where she met her husband, Appolinaire Bakundukize; they have three children.

Christine's sister Clementine and her husband, Didace Kalisa, immigrated to Luxembourg; they have three children.

Christine's sister Clemence immigrated to Belgium; she has two children.

Sister Teya continued to help the most vulnerable groups in Rwanda.

In December 2013, Christine and I returned to Rwanda with several scholars from the University of Notre Dame. We saw firsthand a transformed country, full of hope and life, and emerging as a thriving and prosperous land. We visited several genocide memorials, one of which was the Ntarama memorial in Christine's native Bugesera. One inscription in Kinyarwanda caught our eye. It says: "IF YOU REALLY KNEW ME AND KNEW YOURSELF, YOU WOULD NOT HAVE KILLED ME." It's a quote that sums up the unfortunate fate that fell upon Rwanda. But it's also a wise reflection that carries a message of hope and love and tells us that when we see the good in others, when you "do unto others as you would have them do unto you," love prevails.

Clockwise from top left:

October 1996, Christine's sister Clementine married her fiancé and fellow refuge of the Mille Collines Hotel, Didace Kalisa.

My brother Aimable with his wife, Immaculee, and daughter, Simbi. In 1994 he returned to Rwanda from Burundi to find his parents and several siblings murdered.

Christine's sister, Clemence, who survived at the "valley of death" in Bugesera.

My sister, Julienne, who survived with me at the Swiss Village and the Mille Collines Hotel.

My daughter Carine, her husband, Marcus, and their baby girl, Liana, in Manchester, NH.

My sister Chantal and her son, Steve, who was only two months old when he lost his father in the first weeks of the genocide.

Acknowledgments

I have wanted to write this story ever since Christine and I survived the genocide. I could not have done it without the help I received from my co-author, Dan Groody, C.S.C. Dan, thank you for listening to our story, for your advice and guidance, for the team you put together to visit Rwanda, and for being a part of my journey in writing this book.

To Robert Ellsberg, editor-in-chief and publisher of Orbis Books, thank you for believing in the worthiness of this story, for your valuable advice and editing skills, and for publishing my work. To the team at Orbis Books, thank you for your hard work and your professionalism.

To Colleen Cross, many thanks for your warm welcome at the University of Notre Dame, for your kindness, and for your hard work organizing our trip to Rwanda.

I'm grateful to the scholars and friends who traveled with us to Rwanda from the United States, Switzerland, and Ireland to visit genocide memorials and take time to reflect on some of the spiritual questions that arose from the genocide. Among them were Dan Groody, Virgilio Elizondo, Robert Ellsberg, Jim Shannon, Fulata Moyo, Alan Hilliard, Colleen Cross, and Bill Groody. I thank each and every one of you for your interest in understanding our tragedy and for your resolve to be ambassadors of hope.

To my friend and fellow survivor of the Mille Collines Hotel, Felicien Mutalikanwa, thank you for the warm welcome in Rwanda you and your family extended to our guests; and thanks for your encouragement and your enduring friendship.

To Bridget Martin and Gary Bouchard of *Parable,* the magazine of the Diocese of Manchester, New Hampshire, thank you for your input and advice.

My special thanks to Sister Teya Kakuze and Father Jerome Masinzo for sharing your incredible stories of survival and inalienable faith. Most important, thank you for helping hundreds of traumatized survivors live again and have hope, and for allowing me to be a part of your noble cause.

To the men and women in Rwanda who joined forces to create IBUKA, the umbrella organization that contributed significantly to the rehabilitation of survivors and rebuilding communities, and to various government and nongovernment entities that supported this endeavor, many thanks from the bottom of my heart. I'm appreciative for the work done by everyone and each of you, and for your support during the three-year term I served as president of the organization.

To fellow survivors in Rwanda and abroad who gave me a glimpse into your stories of suffering and survival, thank you for your inspiration and for your commitment to live dignified lives built on the promise of love and tolerance.

My highest appreciation goes to the leadership of the Rwandan Patriotic Front and the United Nations Assistance Mission for Rwanda for organizing our rescue from the Mille Collines Hotel. Thousands of lives were saved thanks to your historic collaboration and your bravery. The same appreciation and thanks go to all individuals, Rwandan and foreigners, who put their lives on the line to save people at risk. I'm particularly indebted to my former neighbor, Therese, for sending my way a guardian angel. I owe her my life and will always be grateful.

To Karen Munsell, thank you for welcoming my family to America and for your moral support; you are a great friend and one of the nicest people I have ever met. Thank you for your friendship and encouragement.

Many thanks to Connie Epich and Robert Drugan for opening your house in Madbury, New Hampshire, and sharing with my family our very first Thanksgiving in the United States. Thank you for the beautiful memories and for being great friends.

To my direct and extended family, thank you for being always there when I needed you the most. Many thanks to my sisters Chantal and Julienne, my brother Aimable, and my in-laws Clemence, Clementine, and Didace; thank you all for your true friendship and encouragement, and for continuing the legacy of love inherited from our beloved parents, gone too soon. My special thanks to Clemence and Chantal for sharing your incredible stories of survival and courage.

To my beautiful daughters Tracy, Chelsea, Fiona, and Carine, thank you for striving to be the best children a parent could wish for. The tragedy that fell upon your grandparents and parents didn't break you. I'm proud of the bright and independent women you have become. Continue to carry the torch of love and hope and be the generation to make our world a better place. I love you more than you can comprehend.

Finally, to my wife, Christine, there is so much I can say about your generous gift of love, but I will simply say thank you. You stood strong beside me when our lives were besieged; you gave me strength and fortified my will to hold on tight to our dreams. Thank you for being the person I can always turn to. Thank you for your love, your humility, and genuine faith. I love you, and I'm so thankful to God for the life we built together.